Clinical Law
for
Clinical Practice

Clinical Law
for
Clinical Practice

Robert Wheeler, FRCS MS LLB(Hons) LLM
Consultant Neonatal and Paediatric Surgeon
and
Associate Medical Director
Department of Clinical Law
University Hospital of Southampton
Southampton Hampshire, England
and
Honorary Senior Lecturer
University of Southampton

CRC Press
Taylor & Francis Group
Boca Raton London New York

CRC Press is an imprint of the
Taylor & Francis Group, an **informa** business

First edition published 2020
by CRC Press
6000 Broken Sound Parkway NW, Suite 300, Boca Raton, FL 33487-2742

and by CRC Press
2 Park Square, Milton Park, Abingdon, Oxon, OX14 4RN

Library of Congress Cataloging-in-Publication Data

Names: Wheeler, Robert (Consultant neonatal and pediatric surgeon), author.
Title: Clinical law for clinical practice / Robert Wheeler.
Description: First edition. | Boca Raton : CRC Press, 2020. | Includes bibliographical
references and index. | Summary: "Clinicians must practice medicine in conformity with
regulatory requirements. That is the daily challenge, and those requirements are founded
on medical law. This book describes how clinical law has been applied in numerous
cases, thus providing a clinical appraisal of the law which is directly applicable to clinical
practice in the United Kingdom"-- Provided by publisher.
Identifiers: LCCN 2020006885 (print) | LCCN 2020006886 (ebook) | ISBN
9780367335595 (paperback) | ISBN 9780367335632 (hardback) | ISBN
9780429320583 (ebook)
Subjects: MESH: Clinical Medicine--legislation & jurisprudence | Patient
Rights--legislation & jurisprudence | Treatment Refusal--legislation &
jurisprudence | Liability, Legal | United Kingdom
Classification: LCC RC46 (print) | LCC RC46 (ebook) | NLM WB 33 FA1 |
DDC 616--dc23
LC record available at https://lccn.loc.gov/2020006885
LC ebook record available at https://lccn.loc.gov/2020006886

ISBN: 978-0-367-33563-2 (hbk)
ISBN: 978-0-367-33559-5 (pbk)
ISBN: 978-0-429-32058-3 (ebk)

Typeset in Times LT Std
by Nova Techset Private Limited, Bengaluru & Chennai, India

Contents

Foreword

It is vitally important that clinical law and clinical practice come together if patients are to get the care that they deserve.

Some lawyers see their discipline as all about rules and find it difficult to understand the complexities of clinical practice. Some clinicians fear that the law will obstruct them from doing the right thing for their patients. It is rare for these perspectives to come together in a way that enables the best of legal and clinical expertise to combine in order to promote high legal and ethical standards in the provision of care. Robert Wheeler is ideally placed to ensure that this happens. He combines experience as a frontline surgeon with legal qualifications. He has long experience in providing practical ethical and legal advice on clinical dilemmas to practising clinicians. He has done this effectively within hospitals and on the national level.

Wheeler brings together in this excellent book accessible explanations of key legal cases in order to help clinicians understand the legal context of their work in terms that make practical sense. It is all too easy for lawyers to explain the principles and rules in ways that seem counter-intuitive to those trying to apply them in healthcare practice. This book places clinical law in its context and shows how it can be made to work for the good of patients.

The way the judgements in the law reports are written often makes it hard for non-lawyers to understand. Long technical explanations of legal doctrine can obscure what is at stake and become impenetrable to the very clinicians who need to understand it. In this book, Wheeler retells the stories of key cases so that the clinically significant elements are brought to the fore and the legal principles and their significance are set out.

This way of explaining the law provides a solid platform to help clinicians to treat their patients properly in all the senses that we hope for: with high clinical standards, consistent with the expectations of the law and in accordance with the demands of clinical ethics and human rights.

Robert Wheeler has provided an excellent resource that bridges the gap that too often opens up between professions of medicine and law. This is Clinical Law *for* Clinical Practice; not in tension with it. That is exactly how it should be.

Sir Jonathan Montgomery
Professor of Health Care Law, University College London
Chair, Oxford University Hospitals NHSFT
Formerly Chair of the Nuffield Council on Bioethics, the Health Research
Authority, and the Human Genetics Commission

Introduction

Has it ever struck you as odd that clinicians abide by rules that they do not understand?

Naturally they accept the framework of anatomy and physiology and pharmacology because that formed the basis of their undergraduate training. For a year or so, that dominated their education, and rightly so. When clinicians hear the urine output has dropped, they revert to glomerular blood flow, loops of Henle and creatinine clearance to find their way to a diagnosis. But Consent? Confidences? Child law? In the absence of 'basic science' training in these fields, how can they possibly divine whether the 14-year-old mother may provide consent for her baby's inguinal herniotomy, and why the father almost certainly cannot? They do not know the answer, but with the benefit of legal 'basic science', they plainly could work it out.

This book starts to fill this lacuna in clinical knowledge with clinical law; wresting back this basic knowledge from the lawyers, while expressing gratitude that the judges and academics who have fashioned the common law (akin to the anatomists, physiologists and pharmacologists who have clarified those other basic sciences for our consumption) so that we can adopt it into the clinical repertoire.

Over the last 10 years, perhaps having coined the phrase 'clinical law', a National Health Service hospital department devoted to this subject has been created. Answering 4000 queries from practitioners regulated by all eight clinical regulators in the United Kingdom, at least we now know the 'frequently asked questions'. Guided by the substance of those topics, judgements in the English (and Welsh and Scottish) courts have been selected and reduced to short bulletins, perhaps 10–20 per year. These have been distributed to the 8000 strong clinical workforce, as well as other organisations. They appear online at https://www.uhs.nhs.uk/HealthProfessionals/Clinical-law-updates/Clinicallawupdates.aspx and are regularly updated, freely available. Sixty of these bulletins (mainly based on judgements handed down over the last 5 years) are presented here.

Although ordered roughly chronologically according to the year the judgement was handed down, the bulletins were issued primarily to serve the clinical needs of the hospital. For this reason, when a clinical question needs urgently to be answered, the chronology is disrupted. As an example, a judgement handed down in 2001 is dealt with midway through the book, responding to a clinical case. This may also explain why sections on generic matters such as 'next of kin' and 'restraint' appear scattered within the text, occasionally unaccompanied by reference to a judgement.

The common law presents a series of stories; each judgement is an opportunity for parties in conflict to seek an impartial adjudication, often as to where the best interests of a citizen who is incompetent or incapacitated might lie. In our experience, going to court is usually cathartic, since both sides in the argument are given a chance fully to express their viewpoints, after which certainty, at the hands of a judge, emerges.

For this reason, patients and parents may be as interested in clinical law as anyone else.

Although most court cases concentrate on the medical aspects of patients' care, the common currencies within clinical law touch on all clinical professions. Physiotherapists take consent every day; pharmacists must protect confidentiality; speech therapists consider the capacity of their patients; nurses wrestle with discussions relating to whether their patients wish to be resuscitated. All eight regulated professions need to be informed of the law properly to treat their patients. Of all the regulators, it is the General Medical Council (GMC) that devotes the most attention to creating materials for its community to use to learn about the legal aspects of practice; this advice is widely applicable across the regulated professions. All of the stories told in this book cover more than one of the 'domains' that the GMC set out, since in reality clinical legal problems are rarely founded on 'single issues'. For that reason, please read this from cover to cover.

Adults Who Refuse Blood

Newcastle Upon Tyne Hospitals FT v LM [2014] EWHC 454 (COP)

In a recent High Court application from Newcastle, a 63-year-old woman (LM), who had been a Jehovah's Witness since the 1970s, was found wandering and confused outside her home; her Hb was 37 on presentation to hospital, where a bleeding duodenal ulcer was diagnosed. Discussing her plight with the gastroenterologists, she was adamant that she did not want treatment with any blood products. They were sure that she had full capacity to make this decision, and that she was aware that she could die without blood transfusion. LM had received other medical treatment over the years, and her adherence to her faith, together with her steadfast refusal of blood in any circumstances, had been regularly and frequently documented in her notes.

The conversation with the gastroenterologists was recorded in the notes, but no formal advanced decision to refuse life-saving treatment existed. Similarly, she had not created a Lasting Power of Attorney enabling refusal of life-saving treatment.

Three days following her discussion with the gastroenterologists, LM deteriorated, requiring intubation, ventilation and sedation. Henceforth, she lacked capacity for further decision-making. Her clinicians felt that transfusion would improve but not guarantee her chances of survival. Perhaps anxious that this woman had not provided a valid advance decision to refuse a life-saving blood transfusion, the clinicians approached the Court of Protection, seeking a declaration that withholding transfusion would be lawful in her case.

The court heard from Mr R, a representative of her congregation, who had known her for 40 years, and who brought with him letters from three other members of the religious group who knew her. R described LM as a formerly active member of the congregation, who fully subscribed to the tenets of the faith (including those opposing blood transfusion) and had taught them to others. Her beliefs on this matter had been consistent. The Trust's position was that LM had made her wishes known, even with the knowledge of impending death. When considering her now, incapacitated, the Trust did not feel that transfusion was in her best interests, since it would be an affront to her established wishes.

The court found that LM had capacity during her early admission to decide whether to accept or refuse a transfusion, and that the advance decision she took prior to losing her capacity (to refuse transfusion) was both valid and applicable to her later more serious condition, when she had lost her capacity. It was therefore lawful to withhold transfusion.

LM died on the day of the judgement.

The judge also noted that he would have granted a declaration even if she had not made a valid applicable decision, since on the facts presented to the court, both from her congregation and the clinicians, a transfusion would not have been in her best interests. This was because her wishes and feelings and long-standing beliefs and values carried determinative weight. It was also relevant that the transfusion might not have been effective in saving her life.

This judgement serves to reinforce the principles of the Mental Capacity Act 2005 (MCA). Adults are presumed to have capacity, but this may be challenged by clinicians should they suspect otherwise. The facts show that LM's clinicians tested her capacity, and found it intact.

The adult patient with capacity is entitled to defend herself against any clinical intervention she chooses to avoid, even if death may result. LM took the opportunity, while she had capacity, to assert her intentions to avoid transfusion. The MCA obliges us when dealing with a patient who lacks capacity to consider, as far as we can ascertain, any past and present wishes expressed by the patient, together with any beliefs and values that would be likely to influence her decision. In so considering her comments made when talking to the gastroenterologists, the Trust concluded that transfusion would not be in her best interests.

Perhaps regrettably, LM was not prompted at that stage to make an advanced decision to refuse a life-saving blood transfusion. If she had done so, her clinicians, it seems, would have been content to rely upon it when she finally lost her capacity due to the progression of her illness. Nevertheless, with the assistance of the Court of Protection (which exists precisely for this eventuality), LM's informal assertions refusing blood were given full weight. Even in their absence, the court made it clear that pleadings from her congregation (together with previous refusals documented in her notes) would have been sufficient to allow the declaration to be made; that blood transfusion would not have been in her best interests.

Thus *Newcastle Upon Tyne Hospitals FT v LM* provides authority for asserting both that (*i*) an advance decision to refuse blood transfusion gives both clinicians and patients some certainty that blood transfusion will be withheld in the prescribed circumstances, and that (*ii*) in the absence of such a formal document, recourse to the Court of Protection (CoP) with substantial informal evidence of the patient's wishes and beliefs can achieve the same result. We should view the CoP as providing an immense benefit to both clinicians and patients, ensuring that the tensions between preserving life and respecting wishes are independently adjudicated.

CHAPTER 2

Discussing the Prospects of Cardiopulmonary Resuscitation

RoA David Tracey v Cambridge NHSFT & Ors [2014] EWCA Civ 822

On 5 February 2011, Mrs Tracey was diagnosed with lung cancer with an estimated life expectancy of 9 months. On 19 February, she sustained a serious cervical fracture after a major road accident. She was admitted to the hospital and transferred to the Neuro-Critical Care Unit under the care of a consultant neurosurgeon. Because she had chronic respiratory problems she was placed on a ventilator, but did not respond to treatment for her chest infection. On 23 and 25 February, efforts were made to wean her from the ventilator, but these were unsuccessful. On 26 February her treatment was reviewed by a consultant intensivist and on 27 February by a consultant oncologist.

The intensivist and oncologist decided that Mrs Tracey should be taken off the ventilator. The question arose as to what would happen if she suffered a cardiorespiratory arrest. On 27 February, a Do Not Attempt Cardiopulmonary Resuscitation (DNACPR) notice was completed. Mrs Tracey was successfully weaned from the ventilator, and her condition appeared to improve. The circumstances in which this DNACPR notice came to be completed and placed in her notes lie at the heart of these proceedings. When one of her daughters discovered that the notice had been made, she was horrified and registered her objections. As a result, the notice was removed and cancelled on 2 March.

Mrs Tracey's condition deteriorated, and she died at 10:38 on 7 March.

The claim against the Trust was that it, among other things breached Mrs Tracey's rights because in imposing the notice, it failed (*i*) adequately to consult Mrs Tracey or members of her family; (*ii*) to notify her of the decision to impose the notice; (*iii*) to offer her a second opinion.

The court found that Mrs Tracey did wish to be consulted about any DNACPR notice that the clinicians were contemplating completing and placing in her notes.

Was it inappropriate to consult in relation to the notice on the facts of this case? The Trust submitted that the intensivist was entitled in the exercise of his clinical judgement to decide not to consult Mrs Tracey on the grounds that (*i*) he believed that CPR would be futile, and (*ii*) he knew that it would cause her distress to be involved in a discussion as to whether she should be resuscitated in the event of a cardiorespiratory arrest.

Further, the Trust submitted that it was inappropriate to involve the patient if the clinician formed the view that CPR would be futile even if he considered that involvement was unlikely to cause the patient harm. The court rejected this submission for two reasons. First, a decision to deprive the patient of potentially life-saving treatment is of a different order of significance for the patient from a decision to deprive them of other kinds of treatment. It calls for particularly convincing justification. The presumption should be that the patient is entitled to know that such an important clinical decision has been taken. The fact that the clinician considers that CPR will not work means that the patient cannot require him to provide it. It does not, however, mean that the patient is not entitled to know that the clinical decision has been taken. Secondly, if the patient is not told that the clinician has made a DNACPR decision, he will be deprived of the opportunity of seeking a second opinion, which may be desirable from the patient's perspective.

In terms of avoiding distress to a patient, the court made two findings that clinicians may not agree with. Firstly, that a belief that it would cause distress to the patient to discuss the issue is unlikely to be sufficient, without more, to make it inappropriate to involve her. The distress must be likely to cause the patient a degree of harm. It was accepted that if the intensivist had given evidence that he did not discuss CPR with her because he thought that she would be distressed and that this might cause her harm, the court would have been most unlikely to interfere with his clinical judgement. In that event, the court would have concluded that the clinician was entitled to decide that it was inappropriate to involve her in the process. The difficulty in this case is that the intensivist gave no such evidence.

The court therefore found that the Trust had violated Mrs Tracey's right to respect for her private life in failing to involve her in the process which led to the DNACPR notice. The court was nevertheless concerned by a 'well-balanced and powerful representation from the Resuscitation Council (RC), expressing the fear that a judgement which states (or implies) that there is a presumption that, save in exceptional cases, every DNACPR decision must be made after consultation with the patient would seriously hamper the ability of health care professionals to provide individualised and compassionate care for vulnerable people towards the end of their lives'. The RC made the further point that in recent years there has been a reduction of inappropriate and unsuccessful attempts at CPR and that a judgement requiring consultation with a patient save in exceptional circumstances would be likely to reverse that process. In suggesting the following formulation, the court hoped that the RC concerns would be largely met:

> 'The clinician has a duty to consult the patient in relation to DNACPR unless he or she thinks that the patient will be distressed by being consulted and that that distress might cause the patient physical or psychological harm'.

It must be emphasised that the court is insisting *only* that we consult before making this decision. Explicitly, the court leaves *the decision* as to whether the DNACPR should be imposed to the doctor.

Our obligation to engage or consult with the patient may be met in a variety of ways. Oral discussion is one; but if you feel that the patient in front of you would find a written note of explanation more helpful, allowing them more time to consider their response (and subsequent questions); then such a note, signed by the consultant in charge of the patient's care might be appropriate.

It should also be noted that the decision in *Tracey* did not specify consultation with the relatives, in circumstances when the patient lacked capacity. However, given the lower likelihood of causing harm or distress to adults accompanying the patient, consulting them before coming to your decision over whether or not to order DNACPR is plainly good practice.

See Chapter 9 for the approach to relatives.

CHAPTER 3

What Should Be Disclosed When Seeking Consent

Montgomery v Lanarkshire [2015] UKSC 11

The Supreme Court has provided clinicians with new guidance relating to what we should disclose to patients when seeking their consent for intervention. The changes are significant, and herald a substantial change to our practice which will likely result in changes to (*i*) what we disclose; (*ii*) how we disclose it; and (*iii*) the way we record the process of obtaining consent.

Mrs Montgomery was an insulin dependent and diabetic woman in the third trimester of her first pregnancy. Educated and articulate, she was concerned about the risks of delivering a large baby vaginally; her obstetrician estimated a birth weight of 3.9 kg at the 36-week scan. At this appointment, the obstetrician noted that Mrs Montgomery was 'worried about [the] size of the baby', and her anxiety that it might be too big for vaginal delivery; it was accepted during the hearing that these concerns had been expressed on previous occasions.

But the obstetrician stated that Mrs Montgomery had not asked her 'specifically about exact risks'. If she had, the obstetrician would have told her of the risks of shoulder dystocia in these circumstances, but since the question was not asked, this risk was not disclosed. This was because the obstetrician viewed the risks of serious injury to this baby as very slight. The obstetrician felt that it was 'fair to allow somebody to deliver vaginally', and that if difficulties were encountered, then recourse would be a caesarean section. Mrs Montgomery accepted this advice. But if she had requested an elective caesarean section, she would have been given one.

The obstetrician gave evidence that diabetic patients who had been advised of the risk of shoulder dystocia would invariably choose caesarean section, and that Mrs Montgomery in particular would have made such an election:

> Since I felt the risk of her baby having significant enough dystocia to cause even a nerve palsy or severe hypoxic damage to the baby was low I didn't raise it with her, and had I raised it with her then yes, she would have no doubt requested a caesarean section, as would any diabetic today.

During the hearings, Mrs Montgomery confirmed that if these risks had been disclosed, she would have considered dystocia a significant risk, and she would have asked for a caesarean section.

During her vaginal delivery, the labour became arrested, and the baby's shoulder became impacted at a point where half of his head was outside the perineum. He survived delivery but has dyskinetic cerebral palsy and Erb's palsy.

The Supreme Court found that Mrs Montgomery had not been informed of her option for a caesarean section; and that if given that option she would have taken it, and delivered a baby without neurological injury. In doing so, the court set out the standard for disclosure that we should use when seeking consent from a patient:

> The doctor ... is under a duty to take reasonable care to ensure that the patient is aware of any material risks involved in any recommended treatment, and of any reasonable alternative or variant treatments. The test of materiality is whether, in the circumstances of the particular case, a reasonable person in the patient's position would be likely to attach significance to the risk, or the doctor is or should reasonably be aware that the particular patient would be likely to attach significance to it.

It should be noted that the 'reasonable' man in this context is a fictional creature who embodies those considerations which ordinarily regulate the prudent conduct of human affairs.

Such a reasonable man or woman provides an objective standard against which the behaviour (of in this case a patient) is compared.

The judgement confirms that not only must we disclose risks that any reasonable patient would wish to consider; but that we should *also* disclose risks that this particular patient in question, who was acting reasonably, would need to know. The fact that the obstetrician accepted that Mrs Montgomery would have '...no doubt requested a caesarean section ...' indicates that she knew that Mrs Montgomery would have sought a caesarean section, even faced with a low risk of harm to the baby. It was for this reason that the court held the disclosure was inadequate and prompts us to tailor our disclosure of risks to the patient in front of us.

Several further points were made in the judgement. First, it was held that the assessment of whether a risk is material *cannot be reduced to percentages*. The significance of a given risk is likely to reflect a variety of factors besides its magnitude: for example, the nature of the risk, the effect which its occurrence would have upon the life of the patient, the importance to the patient of the benefits sought to be achieved by the treatment, the alternatives available, and the risks involved in those alternatives.

Secondly, the doctor's advisory role involves dialogue, the aim of which is to ensure that the patient understands the seriousness of her condition, and the anticipated benefits and risks of the proposed treatment and any reasonable alternatives, so that she is then in a position to make an informed decision. This role will only be performed effectively if the information provided is comprehensible. The doctor's duty is not therefore fulfilled by bombarding the patient with technical information which she cannot reasonably be expected to grasp, 'let alone by routinely demanding her signature on a consent form'.

For this reason, it seems that we will have to depart from the current convention of basing our consent process around a simple form. Rather, we can anticipate that a record of the advice offered, the questions asked and the decisions made will become necessary. It is clear that this will involve much more time than is currently available when seeing outpatients and patients preoperatively. Improving comprehensibility alone will be a significant challenge. It is inevitable that this will mean we will see fewer patients per hour, to allow this dialogue to conclude before the decision to accept or reject the proffered treatment is made.

CHAPTER 4

Deprivation in Essex

Essex County Council v RF&PN&JN&CP [2015] EWCOP 1

Mr CP was a 91-year-old man living alone. He had early dementia but coped at home with assistance. His friends alerted the County Council (CC) to concerns that he was vulnerable to financial exploitation. His niece and nephew told the court that they believed CP's best interests necessitated residential care; not living at home. His niece believed that he would settle in residential care if his friends were not encouraging him to resist leaving his home.

As a result of the concerns of financial exploitation, the Essex CC social worker visited CP on 1 May 2013 and concluded that he lacked the capacity to make decisions about his care, residence and finances. (The court later found that her assessments of his ability to retain, use and weigh information were 'unclear' and that she made no record of his wishes and feelings.) The following day, despite his reluctance and distress, he was taken to a locked dementia unit. This transfer was not lawful, lacking authorisation. The court found that 'it is by no means clear that CP lacked capacity at this time'. When the first Deprivation of Liberty Safeguards (DOLS) authorisation was eventually put in place 2 months later, restrictions on Mr CP's contact with his friends, and his attendance at church, were imposed.

While an agency employee of the council concluded that CP did have capacity to make a decision regarding his accommodation, this was contradicted 2 days later by the social worker. Despite an independent best interests assessor's conclusion that CP had capacity and should be allowed to go home, the same social worker continued to find that he lacked capacity over the ensuing 9 months. During this period, the DOLS authorisation expired in October 2013, again rendering his detention unlawful.

Throughout the whole of CP's detention, he expressed a consistent wish to return home. Yet despite the assessments concluding that he did have capacity, and that returning home was in his best interests, the council did nothing to enable him to do so. He was thus detained unlawfully against his wishes for 17 months.

By the time of the court hearing to extract him from this detention, only his nephew and niece believed that it was in CP's best interests to remain in residential care. The council, the Official Solicitor, the independent nurse specialist and his friends all supported his return home, with a care package that would support his needs.

Mr CP was restored to his home, and substantial damages were awarded.

Unsurprisingly, the court was scathing of CP's management by the County Council. One of the triggers for his removal seemed to have been the concern about the risk of financial abuse. The judge could not understand why his removal and detention in these circumstances were thought to be reasonable or proportionate, or in his best interests. 'Action against the perpetrators would have been preferable to the removal of the victim'.

If CP had been similarly admitted to our hospital, he would have been found to be competent after a correct and complete assessment of his mental capacity. He would have been allowed to go home with support in place. Alternatively, if (as the social worker had done) we had found initially he lacked capacity to make decisions relating to residence, alerted by his friends' and relatives' vehement disagreement as to his best interests, we would have sought DOLS authorisation. On the facts, the DOLS assessors would then have concluded that he had the capacity to return home, despite his relative's protestations.

The DOLS mechanism protects patients from having their rights abused. Providing we employ clinical acumen to ensure that information given to us is scrutinised, ensuring that it is being given in good faith, DOLS serves patients well.

CHAPTER 5

The First Glimpse of a Duty to Warn?

David Spencer v Hillingdon Hospital NHST [2015] EWHC 1058 (QB)

We are all familiar with the necessity to disclose information to patients when we seek their consent for treatment. But when we do so, while we identify (among other matters) the potential risks and complications of the proposed intervention, there has until now been no expectation that we should set out to the patient the signs and symptoms of these potential complications, which would allow the patient to realise that the complication has transpired. But a new court decision provides explicit guidance to clinicians that this is what we should do.

The patient in question was a 49-year-old property service manager who underwent an inguinal hernia repair under general anaesthesia, as a day case.

His body mass index (BMI) was 'just less' than 30; he was otherwise healthy. His surgery was initially laparoscopic, but converted to open after bleeding during the extraperitoneal dissection. The operation time was 53 minutes, and pneumatic boots were applied intraoperatively.

The court found that the patient was told to report 'any problems' postoperatively but was not given any information, oral or written, with respect to the risks or signs and symptoms of venous thromboembolism (VTE).

Following surgery, the patient suffered calf pain and stiffness which he attributed to lack of use; dyspnoea, which he attributed to lack of fitness, and finally unequivocal signs of embolism, leading to his diagnosis and treatment.

The claimant's expert witness criticised the trust for its failure to undertake a formal assessment of the risk of VTE. But he accepted that the patient did not fall into the category of those patients who should be prescribed chemical thromboprophylaxis; since his particular risk of developing deep-vein thrombosis (DVT) was low. The expert nonetheless went on to note that:

> …. all patients undergoing surgery are at some risk and that risk must be addressed by the provision of appropriate advice…. Therefore, there was a basic duty of care to advise Mr Spencer of the symptoms of DVT should it arise in the postoperative period…. As such, the failure by the hospital to advise Mr Spencer of the signs and symptoms of deep vein thrombosis would not be supported by a responsible body of surgical opinion.

The court found that the relevant National Institute for Health and Care Excellence (NICE) guidelines were not wholly clear in identifying the group of patients to which the specific guidance on VTE should be given on discharge. It adopted the claimant's expert witness' view that the NICE guidance (on the provision of information concerning VTE) is intended to be directed at all patients who fall within the groups covered by the guidelines (which would have included the claimant); other than those whose procedure carried no risk, however remote, of DVT or pulmonary embolus.

The court concluded that since pneumatic boots were used to reduce the risk of VTE for all surgical patients under general anaesthetic in the defendant hospital, the use of the boots in the claimant's case was a tacit admission that he fell into the group of patients at risk of this complication. Further, that VTE advice should be given to every patient:

> ….I consider that modern, safe and responsible medical practice should be to give such advice to patients undergoing general anaes-thetic. Whilst in many cases such treatment will cause a small risk of deep vein thrombosis and pulmonary embolism, and one of which many patients will be unaware; to inform such patients of the very particular signs and symptoms of those conditions is a precaution that can save lives and should be given.

Furthermore, the court noted that to expect patients to report 'any problem' was insufficient advice. The claimant's problem of calf pain was too distant from the operative site to expect a reasonable patient to conclude that it could be related to his surgery, and to recognise this sign as 'a problem' in the con-text of the postoperative instruction.

It seems likely that the duty to warn patients so that they can present them-selves early with VTE has arrived. Perhaps we should not be surprised. If an elementary explanation, written or oral, of the signs and symptoms can prevent a patient suffering pulmonary embolus, or dying of one, why would we not provide it?

CHAPTER 6

Can a Patient Choose Her Surgeon?

Kathleen Jones v Royal Devon & Exeter NHSFT
County Court 22 September 2015

Governments encourage patients to believe they have choice, which may extend to the identity of their surgeon. Irrespective of whether this choice is illusory, patients often negotiate this system successfully. The benefits of enabling a patient to choose her surgeon, who is, in turn, pleased that the patient should single them out as a preferred choice, seem self-evident.

Such was the case with Mrs Jones. Suffering from back and claudicating thigh pain, she sought help. After a caudal epidural failed to relieve her symptoms, a local surgeon, Mr C, with a good reputation for spinal surgery was recommended. They met, and she agreed to undergo a bilateral micro-decompression.

As it turned out, Mrs Jones' surgery was to be performed by another surgeon. She was told of this on the morning of the operation. Regrettably, she sustained an intraoperative injury to her cauda equina, giving her a serious chronic neurological injury.

In subsequent litigation, Mrs Jones asserted that if she had been told *before* the day of surgery that she was not going to be operated upon by Mr C, she would not have provided consent.

There were uncertainties and inconsistencies in the evidence of who said what, and when. Nevertheless, the court found that Mrs Jones only learned that Mr C would not be performing the operation 'when effectively she was about to go into theatre'. Expert surgeons providing evidence for both sides agreed that her decision was taken 'so far down the line' that it was unlikely to have been taken freely. The court agreed and accordingly found that the Trust was in breach of its standard of care for obtaining consent.

Previous courts have held that patients have a right to make an informed choice as to whether, and if so when *and by whom* to be operated upon.

The General Medical Council is not so explicit; instructing doctors to disclose to the patient information about 'the people who will be mainly responsible for ... their care, what their roles are'.

This is not a case that establishes for the patient a right to be operated upon by a particular surgeon; it does no such thing. An NHS patient can no more insist on the services of an individual doctor than they can insist on a particular treatment. The case of Mrs Jones does not explore what she would have done after her hypothetical refusal of consent if she had then been faced with yet another surgeon whom she had not chosen. Suppose the chosen one had meantime left the Trust, or retired? Would persistent symptoms have driven her to the pragmatic choice of an alternative surgeon?

This is a case about the **timing** of disclosure. To ensure that patients are free to withhold their consent if they choose, for whatever reason, they should receive the relevant disclosures while free from the coercion of circumstances. If Mrs Jones discovered the identity of her surgeon while on a trolley, in an inadequate gown, rolling towards the theatres, she was vulnerable to coercion. This case therefore also reminds us how important is the judge's evaluation of the unique evidential circumstances (and of the claimant) before them, leading to an outcome no more predictable than that emerging from consultations between patients and their doctors. Quite at what point circumstances coalesce to coerce the patient, preventing them from making a free choice, remains to be seen, as does the influence this decision will have on future cases.

Judges will not answer unasked questions. No one (in *Jones*) asked the court whether it was practicable to ensure that all patients awaiting surgery in England are told in a timely fashion the name of their surgeon, nor the implications that this would have for, among other things, the flexibility of operating lists, and for training surgeons. If this decision was followed, Trusts would have to create a 'metric' ensuring that their standards for the timing of disclosure were reasonable. This is not a measure of quality yet widely addressed in the NHS, nor presumably one for which funds have been allocated.

CHAPTER 7

Sentiments

Wye Valley NHST v Mr B [2015] EWCOP 60

Compulsion may be needed for amputation. Hospitals sometimes seek judicial authorisation for amputations in incapacitated adults. Only an elementary grasp of the concept of human rights is necessary to see that a mutilating procedure should only be imposed against the will of an incapacitated patient after referral to a neutral authority.

Generally, faced with a patient whose life will be lost but for amputation, judges accept that the benefits of the surgery justify its performance and aftermath. During this balancing exercise, courts (and surgeons) are bound by the Mental Capacity Act 2005 to take into account the wishes and feelings and beliefs of the patient concerned. Patients whose lives are immediately dependent on an amputation are generally so obtunded by their illness that their sentiments may not be discernible. Nevertheless, we *all* have a duty to explore the possibility of strongly held wishes or beliefs with those who accompany the patient, or in their absence an Independent Mental Capacity Advocate. Previous utterances during the time they had capacity may illuminate the patient's attitude to amputation.

The court was confronted with Mr B, 73 years old, with a putrefying foot, diabetes, and schizophrenia. He had only days to live without surgery. A judgement emerged that should be read by any surgeon who has to make decisions in the best interests of others.

Mr B had for 50 years been guided by (what his doctors described as) delusions; of angelic voices, and the voice of the Virgin Mary. The voices had discouraged him from taking medications, perhaps accounting for his poor compliance with antipsychotic (and latterly hypoglycaemic and antibiotic) medications. His surgeons, faced with systemic sepsis originating from uncontrolled osteomyelitis, were able only to persuade Mr B to acquiesce to changes of his dressing. He utterly dismissed the offer of amputation.

The judge met Mr B, obtaining a deeper understanding of his view of the world, and of his 'fierce independence'. He was satisfied that Mr B did not have the capacity to make treatment decisions about his foot, since he had only limited understanding of the information and was unable to weigh the relevant evidence in coming to a decision. But Mr B had consistently opposed amputation over the entire period of the year that it had been under discussion.

In his conversation with the judge, Mr B made plain his views on surgical interference, the prospects of death, his entry into heaven, his refusal of nursing homes and conserving his leg. These wishes and feelings and religious beliefs were sufficiently long-standing to be integral to him. The judge noted that to think of Mr B without his illnesses and idiosyncratic beliefs would be no more meaningful than to think of an 'unmusical Mozart.'

The weight that should be accorded to an incapacitated person's beliefs and wishes and feelings was discussed in court. The Trust pleaded that the views expressed by a person who lacked capacity could be considered to have less weight than those expressed by a person with capacity. The judge firmly disagreed, holding that wishes and beliefs and values and feelings are as important to the incapacitated person as they are to anyone else. Arguably, more so.

Mr B's religious sentiments were certainly of enormous importance to him. Concluding that there is no theoretical limit to the weight (or lack of weight) that should be given to an incapacitated person's wishes, beliefs, values and feelings; the judge found that it would be unlawful to perform the amputation in the face of Mr B's opposition.

Mr B was unusually clear in his sentiments. Their long-standing nature, together with the role they had played in the fabric of his life was persuasive. The weight accorded to them provided an unusual result, since in most cases, applications to declare amputation lawful in these circumstances will succeed. Nevertheless, this is an important reminder that despite their lack of capacity, a person's wishes, beliefs and feelings may be enough to persuade surgeons (or courts) that palliation, not intervention, is in their patient's best interests.

CHAPTER 8

Unwise Decisions

Kings College Hospital NHSFT v C & V [2015] EWCOP 80

Patients do not often disagree with the clinician who is treating them. When disagreement occurs, under some circumstances, this may lead to the patient's capacity to make decisions being questioned. It is natural to sympathise with the clinician who is dismayed by the patient who rejects advice that to bystanders would seem obviously consistent with that patient's best interests. This is never more relevant than when life is at stake. When a patient is refusing life-saving treatment, a nurse or doctor may question whether the person has capacity to make this decision; deducing that a refusal of life-saving treatment may denote an inability to understand, retain and weigh the relevant information. Diagnosing such inabilities, if combined with an impairment or disturbance of the patient's mind or brain, would confirm their incapacity. If the patient lacks capacity, a decision will be taken in his or her best interests as to whether life-saving treatment should be given; and the starting presumption would be in favour of preserving life.

A woman in her early fifties, C, was facing a course of renal dialysis, estimated to be required for only 6–12 weeks. Three 4-hour sessions each week would be needed. Without this treatment, she would quickly die; but with treatment, the outlook for her unsupported renal function was 'cautiously optimistic'. C's renal failure was acquired as a result of attempted suicide with paracetamol, but by the time of the hearing, her concomitant liver failure was resolving, and she was otherwise healthy.

C's adult life was 'characterised by impulsive and self-centred decision-making without guilt or regret; living her life entirely and unapologetically on her own terms. That life revolved largely around her looks, men, material possessions and living the "high life"'. In her evidence, one of her daughters, making it plain to the court that her mother was dear to her, nevertheless had learnt to accept her mother for what she was:

> My mother's values, and the choices that she made have always been based on looks (hers and other people's), money, and living (at all costs) what she called her 'sparkly' lifestyle … her life was, from her

point of view, a life well lived. I have never known her express regret, or really take responsibility for anything, including the choices she has made.

In these circumstances, was C's decision to refuse renal replacement therapy an indicator of her incapacity to make such a judgement? On the evidence presented, the court found that C had capacity to decide whether or not to consent.

In doing so, the judge reminded us that the patient's right to choose whether or not to consent to medical treatment is not confined to making decisions that others might regard as sensible. The right to choose is not dependent upon the patient's *reason for making the choice* being rational, or sensible, or even known. It is an uncomfortable thought that C rejected life despite the knowledge that some weeks of dialysis would enable her restoration to a quality of life enjoyed by countless survivors of an acute kidney injury. You may conclude that her choice was not sensible, rational or correct.

There is a temptation to base a judgement of a person's capacity upon whether they seem to have made a good or bad decision, and in particular on whether they have accepted or rejected medical advice, but this temptation must be avoided. To succumb to it would be to allow 'the tail of welfare to wag the dog of capacity'. In other words, doctors and nurses should not allow their (laudable and humane) instinct for giving the patient a good outcome to override evidence establishing a patient's capacity. To do otherwise risks infringing the rights of that group of persons who, although vulnerable, are still capable of making their own decisions. This is particularly true of patients who despite suffering mental illness are able to make decisions about their medical treatment.

A capacitous adult is entitled to make a decision relating to treatment, notwithstanding its wisdom.

CHAPTER 9

Consulting Relatives

Elaine Winspear v City Hospitals Sunderland NHSFT [2015] EWHC 3250 QB

We are now well aware that in England and Wales, a decision that anticipates withholding cardiopulmonary resuscitation (CPR) when a patient's heart or breathing stops must be discussed with them beforehand. This obligation is important, because it allows the patient to bring to our attention matters to which we, as clinicians, are almost certainly oblivious. The patient may be days away from the maturity of an insurance policy, earmarked as an essential support for the family's finances; or perhaps a wedding or birth is imminent, at which the patient regards herself as an essential guest. The prospect of remaining alive for these events may be, for the patient, a sufficient benefit to make the risk of enduring CPR acceptable.

This revelation will not necessarily sway our decision as to whether CPR is appropriate; it is the doctor, not the patient, who is the decision-maker in these circumstances. But it is self-evidently essential that we consider the patient's wishes in this respect. If the patient so requests, we should provide them with a second opinion with respect to the advisability of CPR.

There is a qualification to this duty. If we believe that the discussion relating to withholding CPR will cause not just distress to the patient, but also harm, we may avoid it.

To what extent does this duty to discuss resuscitation apply to relatives, when the patient lacks the capacity to contribute? The mother of 28-year-old Carl Winspear claimed that his human rights were breached, because she was not consulted over the Do Not Attempt Cardiopulmonary Resuscitation (DNACPR) decision made about him. He had cerebral palsy and had been admitted to hospital with pneumonia, necessitating oxygen, fluids and antibiotics, lacking capacity to discuss his possible needs for resuscitation.

After his admission to the ward at 19.00, Carl's mother went home at 21.00, called the ward again at 22.00, and went to bed. The registrar looking after her son considered that his severe kyphosis and flexion contractures made the performance of effective CPR impossible. The registrar asserted that 'he did not want to inflict a treatment that was distressing, painful and undignified because it had no chance of success'. Accordingly, he entered *'DNACPR. Speak to family in the morning'* in the notes.

Explaining why he did not first discuss his decision with Carl's mother, the registrar did not think Carl had a high risk of deterioration overnight; although he was unwell, he was stable. He delayed filling in the prescribed DNACPR form until the opportunity to discuss the decision with Ms Winspear arose later that morning.

Following a conversation with Carl's mother shortly before midday, the order was cancelled. Subsequently, it was explained that artificial ventilation was unsuitable, because he would be unlikely ever to be weaned off it. His condition deteriorated that evening, and he died of bronchopneumonia at 23.05.

The litigation that followed concerned only the lack of consultation with his mother; no criticism was levelled at the clinical decision itself.

The court found that in the circumstances, it would have been appropriate to discuss the proposed decision with Carl's mother; it was plainly important; she had been Carl's lifelong carer; she had travelled into hospital with him and had remained in contact while at home. All of this established her 'credentials' as an interested relative. It was also practicable for the registrar to contact her by telephone at 03.00, to discuss the proposed decision, before the DNACPR notice had been appended to her son's notes. Accordingly, Carl's rights had been breached by the failure to consult with his mother, before the final decision over his resuscitation status had been made.

This case provides explicit guidance. We must discuss proposed DNACPR decisions with the relatives of incapacitated patients, providing it is appropriate and practicable to do so, before the decision is made. The caveat permitting us not to engage in this discussion if it will cause harm to the patient does not apply to his or her relatives.

CHAPTER 10

Doctrine of Double Effect

R v Adams [1957] Crim LR 365
R v Cox [1992] 12 BMLR 38
R v Woollin [1999] 1 AC 82

It is inevitable that we cause our patients harm during our attempts to deal with their disease or symptoms. Ubiquitous examples of harm are incision, amputation, organ removal, cellular poisoning or irradiation, all of which would be criminal acts outside the control of the clinical regulators. This dilemma of a double effect, where harm coexists with benefit, is stark when considering the use of powerful analgesics for pain relief. Palliation of pain is essential for the patient's well-being, but it is foreseeable that due to the palliation, the patient's life may be shortened.

In 1957, Dr Bodkin Adams was charged with the murder of one of his patients by administration of morphine. She was an elderly woman who had suffered a stroke. Dr Adams had administered increasing doses of opiates, to 'relieve her sensation of pain'. The judge held that doctors could take all necessary steps to relieve pain and suffering, even if the measures taken may incidentally shorten life. The jury acquitted Dr Adams, presumably because they found that he was seeking only to relieve pain, only incidentally accelerating death.

Thirty-five years later, Dr Cox, treating a woman who was '...terminally ill with rheumatoid arthritis, in considerable pain, if not agony...', had administered two ampoules of intravenous undiluted potassium chloride a minute or so before she died. During his trial for her homicide, the judge told the jury that it was plainly the doctor's duty to do all that was medically possible to alleviate pain and suffering. His defence asserted that this was an unorthodox method of relieving pain and suffering, which the patient's clinical picture fully justified. Dr Cox was convicted.

The defence had failed to convince the jury that the doctor's intention had solely been to relieve his patient's suffering. It can be deduced from the conviction that they believed he intended to kill her. If he had chosen a conventional analgesic, both the prosecution and the conviction would have been unlikely.

The core requirement of the doctrine of double effect is the absence of an intention to kill. If such an intention is present, the motivation of the clinician is irrelevant. Irrespective of the desire to abbreviate suffering, this beneficial motivation is washed away by the law's insistence that a person who carries out their intention to kill (outside the lawful excuses that would include warfare) must face the charge of murder.

Unsurprisingly, critics of the doctrine assert that it is impossible that a clinician could ignore the foreseeable consequences of administering an opiate: Notwithstanding the relief of suffering, death due to respiratory depression would surely be predictable? Accordingly, how can we distinguish foresight from intent? Why wouldn't the malicious clinician, privately intending death, conceal his motive by asserting the obvious defence of double effect?

In the trial of a man for murder (Woollin had, in furious temper, thrown his baby onto a hard surface, fracturing the skull, killing the infant), it was held that a consequence (death) could be said to be intentional if the defendant foresaw it was 'virtually certain' that it would arise.

Applying this to clinical law, it can be seen that no reasonable doctor or nurse would administer a drug or a dose which they considered (with virtual certainty) would lead to the patient's death.

Accordingly, since in reasonable clinical practice the foresight of death due to the administration will not approach the threshold of 'virtual certainty', legal academics, doctors and judges now agree that the doctrine of double effect is manageable in the courts.

We remain unfettered in our ability to palliate pain, provided we have no intention whatsoever to end the patient's life in doing so. But as soon as an intention to kill is allowed to subvert the intention to palliate, murder ensues.

CHAPTER 11

Needle Phobia

Re L (Patient: Non-Consensual Treatment) [1997] 2 FLR 837
Re MB (Medical Treatment) [1997] 2 FLR 426

Twenty years ago, English courts were twice faced with the dilemma of
needle phobia; both cases relating to women who had consented to urgent
caesarean section and explicitly wanted their babies to be born safely. In one,
L was in full-term obstructed labour, while MB had a footling breach presentation in a 33-week-old baby.

Neither woman would consent to the venous cannulation required for the
anticipated anaesthesia, because they were both terrified by the prospect of an
injection.

In the first case, the judge ruled that L had demonstrated capacity to consent
for the operation. But he found that her extreme needle phobia amounted to
an involuntary compulsion, disabling her from weighing and balancing treatment information, and thus removing her capacity to refuse the procedure.
Her phobia compelled L 'with such force that her own life would be in serious peril'. Accordingly, he declared that it was lawful for L to be cannulated,
since in her (temporarily) incapacitated state, safe delivery of her baby was in
her best interests.

In the case of MB, on similar facts, a High Court judge again declared that
it would be lawful to compel her to have the treatment required for a safe
delivery. An appeal was immediately launched, but the Court of Appeal dismissed this in the early hours of the following morning. The court started by
reminding itself that a person with capacity is entitled to make a decision for
religious or other reasons, for rational or irrational reasons, or for no reasons
at all, irrespective of the consequences. Irrationality was described in stark
and memorable terms:

> A decision so outrageous in its defiance of logic or of accepted moral
> standards that no sensible person who had applied his mind to the
> question to be decided could have arrived at it.

The Court of Appeal accepted that panic, irrationality and indecisiveness may be symptoms of incapacity, but made it clear that by themselves, these do not amount to a loss of capacity (as today is defined by the Mental Capacity Act 2005). The court reiterated the proposition that needle phobia amounts to an involuntary compulsion, asserting that '...temporary factors, such as confusion, shock, fatigue, pain or drugs, or panic induced by fear might erode or destroy capacity'. It emphasised that careful examination of the evidence was required before concluding whether fear had destroyed capacity; as opposed to being a reason for capacitous refusal. Applying these principles to MB's facts, it was held that she had lost her capacity because her needle phobia had dominated her thinking.

Adults with capacity have dominion over their decision-making for consent to any intervention. It is only in extraordinary circumstances that this principle can be challenged. Nevertheless, most clinicians will see needle phobia in their career. In elective or urgent circumstances, it should be possible to anticipate the destruction of the patient's capacity due to fear, and negotiate a solution prior to the start of the intervention.

In emergencies, it would be rare for needle phobia to have an opportunity to erode the patient's capacity to consent for treatment. Most patients are usually very unwell in the prelude to their emergency intervention. The illness itself may have rendered them incapacitated; or at the very least, the severity of their plight prior to surgery or other procedure may overshadow the panic that the prospect of cannulation might induce in less onerous circumstances. But should needle phobia stand in the way of emergency treatment in a patient who otherwise has capacity, it would seem likely that a telephone application to the High Court at any time of the day or night will produce a similar result to that in these two obstetric cases.

CHAPTER 12

Candid over Complications

No case

When something has gone wrong during clinical management, it is now commonplace to expect that the patient or their relatives will be informed of what it was that went wrong, and what the consequences of this event might be. In this way, the duty of candour imposed by the General Medical Council (GMC) (among other regulators) is fulfilled.

To what extent, if at all, are the 'complications' that the patient may endure caught by the same obligation? This is most clearly demonstrated by examples from surgery, although the principles can be applied to other clinical circumstances.

Surgeons are accustomed to disclosing to their patients that the proposed operation may go wrong. The disclosure of 'bleeding and infection' is ubiquitous across the land, together with the more specific foreseeable risks, such as damage to contiguous structures, recurrence of the original diagnosis or inadvertent exacerbation of disease. Failure to disclose these foreseeable complications prior to surgery, particularly if they then maim or paralyse or scar the patient, may lead to a claim that the consent was invalid and that the patient, had they known of the risk, would have either never had the operation, or would have had it performed by somebody else at another time.

Since all of these misadventures are plainly caught by the GMC's threshold of 'something going wrong', they would need to be reported to the patient by the candid surgeon if they crystallise during surgery. Merely because the division of a ureter during hysterectomy appears as a foreseeable complication on a consent form cannot negate the duty to be candid should it occur; it is plainly an example of something going wrong.

This class of surgical complication must be starkly distinguished from the complications of the disease itself, since these are explicitly excluded from the duty of candour. The patient awaiting surgery for her rectal cancer might present with venous thromboembolism. This is a regrettable complication of her disease, but by itself cannot lead to the deduction that something has gone wrong with surgical management. Accordingly, there would be no duty to be candid.

By contrast, if the same patient, if arriving thrombus-free for her resection, then had a postoperative venous thromboembolism, because the unit's protocol of 28 days of low-molecular-weight heparin was not prescribed, a duty of candour would certainly be owed. Since something went wrong.

In clinical practice fault is *not* determinative when considering whether to be candid over the occurrence of a complication. Thus clinicians will wish to ensure that the patient is made aware of events to which she may otherwise remain oblivious, since this information may have an effect on her subsequent decision-making. Accordingly, if something goes wrong which causes a complication, irrespective of whether the 'thing that went wrong' is indicative of substandard care, our obligation to be candid about the existence of the complication persists. The question of whether fault has occurred, and whether it has caused the complication, is likely to require careful consideration. Clinicians, and those in the hospital who advise them, need to be certain of the facts before being candid, to ensure that they do not mislead the patient when fulfilling their duty of candour. It is likely that candour relating to fault and causation, while eventually necessary, may only be possible after an investigation of the event leading to the complication is concluded.

CHAPTER 13

Examining Patients with Their Consent

No case

In the United Kingdom, all operations performed within any surgical speciality under general anaesthesia require consent from patients with capacity, or are performed only in the best interests of those without capacity, in terms set out within the General Medical Council's guidance from 2008.

To this group of procedures that require consent should be added any other interventions performed on the patient while conscious that would not, in normal circumstances, be performed by a person without a clinical qualification or training.

In this way, the patient's consent legitimises an act that they entrust to a practitioner *because* the practitioner is a clinician. In this way, our clinical regulators provide patients with a degree of certainty that the operator is capable of performing the procedure.

It is less easy to set a threshold above which consent is required for simple physical examination. It has always been the case that seeking permission to examine a patient has been considered an exercise in basic good manners. Striding into the room, pulling back the sheets and placing the cold examining hand on the surprised abdomen without uttering a word is now unacceptable. Bearing in mind that valid consent is based on what the reasonable person would want to know, little needs to be disclosed. 'May I examine your tummy?' generally suffices for disclosure … and the oral agreement is quite enough. No forms or records are required – just civilised behaviour. In living memory, vaginal and rectal examinations were performed without consent on anaesthetised patients solely for the purpose of teaching. This is no longer permitted, but if digital rectal or vaginal examination is foreseeable during a procedure under general anaesthetic, should explicit consent be obtained?

It is unlikely that any surgeon would attempt such an examination in the conscious patient without obtaining their consent. Why would you not do so preoperatively? It will not involve significant revelations; you need to do a rectal because the anal canal and lower rectum must be evaluated; complications are unlikely, and if they occur, they will be transient. There is no practicable alternative to this invasion.

This will not make the overall disclosure for surgery or its record significantly more onerous. It would seem prudent, on the same grounds, to disclose the need for a foreseeable urinary catheter, and record the forthcoming consent.

Meanwhile, in the outpatients, should the patient's consent for rectal be recorded? There is ample evidence in the press that predators, including surgeons, have used their influential status unlawfully to commit intimate assaults. If you would rather establish evidence that you had obtained oral consent from the patient, you could, without difficulty, include that fact in the notes, or in the letter that recorded the consultation. It seems probable that employing Trusts (and private hospitals) may soon decide that this practice is essential for their own protection, if not for that of their employees.

And the hinterland between examination and surgery? Venepuncture, venous and arterial cannulae, chest drains and lumbar punctures; all plainly require oral consent, but the complexity of the necessary disclosure varies widely according to the circumstances. For this reason, there is wide variation of attitudes to recording this oral consent that all fall within the bounds of reasonable practice. A simple rule is to record in proportion to complexity. A patient's oral consent for routine venepuncture will rightly go unrecorded (unless their religion solemnly forbids blood-letting). But faced with a coagulopathic patient who would only marginally benefit from a chest drain, the balancing act between risk and benefit could lead to stark choices. Here, recording the disclosure and consent on a form might seem prudent. As always, a matter for clinical judgement.

CHAPTER 14

Covert Treatment

AG v BMBC & SNH [2016] EWCOP 37

Vets do this all the time. Faced with the stark prognosis of a beloved family friend with 'Cushing's' who will die unless he gets his daily bromocriptine, the vet recommends without qualms that the horse's owner conceal the foul-tasting tablet by burial deep within a carrot. Otherwise, presented with the undisguised drug, the horse would invariably reject it, dying a metabolic death. The benefits of covert treatment are uncontroversial and plainly outweigh the disadvantages in these circumstances. Following the same doctrine, parents who must get antibiotics into a toddler blithely conceal the medication in spoonfuls of jam.

Yet such deceit, practised by a doctor upon an adult with capacity, would be construed as an affront to the adult's right to choose which medicines to take, if any at all. For any medicine with noxious side effects, the foreseeable consequences of covert administration to an adult with capacity include the grave criminal charge of poisoning. Covert treatment in the shadow of these threats to reputation, employment and liberty seems immediately an unattractive prospect, even when executed with good intentions.

Covert treatment of an adult with capacity is unlawful (at the very least) because there is no consent. Covert treatment of incapacitated adults is probably regularly and frequently practised and justified by the practitioners as in the patients' best interests. But reported cases are very rare and consequently little instruction on the subject is available.

Twenty years ago, the *British Medical Journal* reported a case where to calm a disturbed 'physically strong' 91-year-old man, threatening his doctor with a walking frame, haloperidol concealed in a cup of tea was used to resolve the confrontation. The commentary asserted that this patient was 'cognitively intact' (but was written in an era when the formal diagnosis of incapacity was still developing, so whether he had capacity is unknowable). The patient's recurrent episodes of bombastic 'hypomania' were eventually diagnosed as temporal lobe epilepsy, and anticonvulsant therapy coincided with cessation of these attacks. While the relevant regulators accepted that from the clinicians' perspective this covert treatment was lawful, those governing the hospital sought a formal undertaking from the doctor that the practice of covert medication would not be repeated. Perhaps the Board considered that a compulsory injection into a physically restrained patient was preferable.

In the recent case of AG it transpired that a 92-year-old woman, whose dementia had destroyed her capacity to make decisions for herself, was being given thyroxine and diazepam covertly, without which, the court heard, she would become severely unwell, both mentally and physically. The court took the unusual step of setting out guidance for covert treatment of incapacitated adults.

This includes full consultation with clinicians and family and explicit authorisation under the Mental Capacity Act 2005 (and its associated Deprivation of Liberty Safeguards), together with a regular review of the decision to administer medications covertly.

This judgement is welcomed. It permits clinicians who follow the guidance to provide humane covert treatment to incapacitated adults, while ensuring that they are not tainted with the hint of complicity in an unauthorised deception of vulnerable patients, whose care has been entrusted to them.

CHAPTER 15

Can Blood Be Compulsorily Administered under the Mental Health Act 1983?

Nottinghamshire Healthcare NHST v RC [2014] EWCOP 1317

The question as to whether an Advance Decision to Refuse Treatment (ADRT) can be used to refuse blood transfusion was answered in a case heard in 2014. But in the same year the different question of whether transfusion could be given compulsorily was also addressed. This concerned RC, 23 years old, who at the time of the court hearing was in a secure psychiatric hospital. He had been transferred there from prison, where he was serving a 5-year sentence for a serious assault. In February 2014, RC deliberately lacerated his brachial artery and had since attempted to reopen that wound a number of times. This led to his compulsory admission to the secure hospital a month later, together with the use of a restraint belt to prevent him slashing the artery.

The court found that RC suffered from a personality disorder rendering him antisocial and emotionally unstable. He cut himself with the intention of providing a distraction from distressing thoughts and feelings, particularly when severely distressed. The court held that at least on some occasions RC had full capacity to harm himself; furthermore, it held that RC took the view that it 'is his body and therefore his choice to damage it'. In April 2014, 3 weeks after admission to the psychiatric hospital, RC signed an ADRT, which was in turn properly witnessed. It provided that no transfusions of blood or primary blood components should be administered to him in any circumstances, even if his life were at risk. This accorded with an earlier trenchant refusal of blood transfusion after his arterial injury in February.

Anticipating the inevitability of further self-inflicted vascular injuries, the secure hospital Trust sought, among other things, a declaration that RC had the capacity to refuse blood products and that his ADRT was valid and operative, should the situation arise where RC needed transfusion but was incapable (for any reason) of issuing a decision to refuse one.

The court found that an adult of a sound mind (with respect to this particular decision) was entitled to refuse medical treatment, and that this right was not diminished by his status as a detained prisoner. In addition, since the judge was 'perfectly satisfied' that RC had full capacity in April when he executed the ADRT, should he ever be in the position where, for whatever reason, he is incapacitated, and a blood transfusion is indicated, then his advance decision will be operative.

It is not surprising that ADRTs for mental illness are rendered ineffective if and when a patient comes under the scope of Part IV of the Mental Health Act 1983, which gives authority to compel a capacitous person to have such treatment. After all, if refusal of treatment were possible, patients with relapsing mental illness could choose to avoid the compulsion inherent in the Mental Health Act 1983, in part, defeating its purpose.

Section 63 of the Act provides for, among other things, compulsory treatment of physical disease only if this is a symptom or manifestation of the mental illness for which the patient has been compulsorily detained. Lacerations inflicted as a result of delusory psychotic beliefs would be included in this, so compulsory treatment of RC's brachial artery injury could be provided lawfully, if necessary, despite RC's capacitous refusal. The judge considered whether, in addition to suturing the laceration, blood transfusion to correct RC's resultant anaemia could also be compulsorily administered.

Although an ADRT can be overridden if treatment under section 63 is required, the facts of RC's case were considered by the judge to be 'highly relevant'. The judge went further, finding that to '…impose a blood transfusion would be a denial of a most basic freedom … an abuse of power even to think about imposing a blood transfusion … that he presently had capacity to refuse'. This illustrates the point that section 63 gives discretion to impose compulsory treatment upon the patient, but it does not compel the doctor to treat if they feel this is disproportionate or unnecessary.

From RC's perspective this was a just result. While the court found that blood transfusion could be administered compulsorily under section 63 of the Act, it was also held that the highly relevant facts of his case made it unjust to use this legal power to force RC to have blood.

In finding that blood transfusion could be considered a treatment for mental disorder in this context, the judge extended the remit of compulsory treatment. Treatment of the long-term *consequences* of injury has not, until RC's case, been compellable under section 63. The courts had hitherto been fastidious in restricting the extent that physical illness can be treated under mental health legislation. Paracetamol overdoses, if caused by a depressive illness, can be compulsorily treated in the sectioned patient with activated charcoal, intending to reduce the biological burden of the drug, but no one has ever suggested compulsorily dealing with subsequent hepatic replacement therapy under the Mental Health Act. Liver damage caused by paracetamol is analogous to anaemia caused by arterial injury. Deciding whether a blood transfusion should be imposed under section 63 may be a more complex exercise than this judgement suggests.

CHAPTER 16

Genetic Confidentiality

ABC v St George's Healthcare NHSFT [2015] EWHC 1394 QB;
see Chapter 62 for most recent review of case

Cases from unusual sources have recently given us considerable insight into the English courts' perspective of the confidential relationship between the doctor and her patient. We all recognise that confidentiality is an imperative, rather than merely an option, in the exercise of good manners, but quite how far will the courts ask us to go in protecting our patients' secrets?

This story starts with an unlawful killing. The man responsible, F, was convicted of his wife's manslaughter, because he lacked capacity to form the intention necessary to be found guilty of murder. Once placed in a secure psychiatric unit, it was suspected that F might have Huntington's disease (HD). This would go some way to explaining his lack of capacity to form the intention to murder; although his capacity to defend his private information was intact. At the relevant tertiary genetic centre, the responsible triplet repeat of the gene for HD was confirmed. F said that he had told his brother, and his doctors sought consent to disclose the diagnosis to his daughter, who at this time was in her first trimester, attending the same tertiary centre for her antenatal care. F refused consent for his daughter to be told, in part because he feared it might lead her to have an abortion. Her later complaint, the substance of this case, was that if she had been told of her father's diagnosis, she would have been tested, since her inheritance risk was 50%. The test would have revealed her own diagnosis of HD. And on the basis of that, she asserted that she would have aborted her fetus, thus obliterating the risk of transmitting to another generation this grievous disease.

The case was discontinued because the judge refused to accept that the hospital's duty of care to the father extended to a third party, in this case his daughter. To find otherwise would have been invidious, since the geneticists would have had to choose between their duties of confidence to the father, as opposed to their duty to disclose to the daughter. By making either choice, they would have broken their duty of care to one or the other patient.

But putting that aside, the judge made crystal clear the duty to protect the father's confidence, irrespective of the consequences to his oblivious child and grandchild.

A year later, a Family Court sitting in private was considering care proceedings relating to a 15-year-old girl. A psychiatrist who had assessed and treated her mother provided factual evidence relating to her mental health to the court. Following the care proceedings, the mother made allegations in the press against, among other things, Dr X's conduct, and she published materials on the Internet despite an injunction preventing her from doing so. The materials she put in the public domain included both defamatory statements about Dr X and an excerpt from her own medical report.

Doctor X was unable to defend himself in this (very) public arena without disclosing the patient's clinical information, necessary to counter these criticisms point by point.

He returned to the Family Court, requesting to use her clinical details to defend himself via 'reputable journalists'. This, he said, was necessary, since '... misinformed press reporting has severely damaged my reputation and my ability to work in child protection or within the court arena'.

The court would not allow this, irrespective of his argument that the mother had already willingly placed her private information into the public domain. The court reminded Dr X that the mother's behaviour gave him no licence to behave similarly. If he wished to assert that her accusations were defamatory, he was free to do so in the civil courts. But emphatically he was not permitted to join in open public combat with the mother armed with her very personal confidences.

Both cases illustrate that even with health and reputations at stake, courts are loathe to allow confidences to be shared without consent, despite circumstances that some may see as favouring disclosure on the basis of 'natural justice'. Whether or not you agree with these judgements, their defence of confidence is plainly resolute and will bolster our regulator's determination to maintain patient confidentiality.

Postscript: Please see case in Chapter 62.

CHAPTER 17

Refusing Hospital Discharge

Barnet Primary Care Trust v X [2006] EWHC 787 QB
Sussex Community NHSFT v Price [2016] EWHC 3167 QB

It is not uncommon to hear of the patient with capacity who resists hospital discharge but who has no medical cause to remain. Their reasons are legion, but when all is said and done, they would rather stay in your hospital than return either to their home or to another National Health Service establishment. You will probably be accustomed to the ensuing difficulties when trying in a kindly, dignified and humane fashion to discharge them, thus making way for a patient who needs treatment. This is rarely straightforward.

The English courts have rarely been involved in the process of ensuring that unwilling patients leave hospital, but on the occasions they are, useful principles are established. In 2006, a case was decided where a man was originally admitted (in December 2002) with a 1-week history of declining mobility and lumbar pain. Further investigation revealed stenosis of his spinal canal, although intervention was neither provided nor required, other than a splint for foot drop. A 7-year history of substantial bilateral groin hernias was also noted, causing discomfort and some difficulties with micturition. The risks of hernia surgery outweighed the benefits, and an expectant approach was prescribed, both by surgeons and anaesthetists. By May 2003, an 'expectant' clinical approach was established, and his subsequent stay in hospital until the hearing in 2006 was prolonged only by his unwillingness to go home.

There was no medical reason for his continuing admission, other than for two brief chest infections coinciding with his residence in the hospital. The chest infections reflected moderately severe chronic obstructive respiratory disease, for which the latter required no medical intervention necessitating residential care. During 2004, the question of operation for his hernias was revisited, the patient asserting that he should have the choice as to whether he would have a repair, and noting that he would welcome death as a complication … the surgeons were not persuaded to operate.

It was accepted by all that his home was uninhabitable. The hospital authorities (who were pleading to repossess the bed on the ward that he was occupying) had identified residential homes that agreed to take him and could supply the limited social care he required. Evidence from the ward manager confirmed that he required only minimal assistance with the activities of daily living, and thus either sheltered accommodation or residential care would be suitable for him. But the patient would not engage in this process, maintaining the view that he needed treatment in hospital.

The court was satisfied that the hospital had done all it reasonably could to make possible this man's orderly discharge from hospital, that the hospital had no alternative other than apply for repossession, and that the patient had taken no opportunity to contradict the hospital's evidence. The existence of alternative arrangements, in the form of residential homes willing to look after the patient, meant that there was no breach of his human rights. The court ordered the patient to leave hospital within 14 days and imposed upon him £10,000 in costs.

This year a case has emerged with similar facts. A woman originally requiring orthopaedic surgery was admitted in August 2015 to a rehabilitation unit, but by November she needed no nursing care and was refusing all therapy. However, she claimed her mobility had not improved sufficiently for her to leave. She had refused to communicate either with the Trust or the local council and refused to provide relevant information which might have enabled other care arrangements to be put in place. The patient did not instruct lawyers to oppose the Trust's plea to repossess her room, and the court found that there was no medical reason why she should not return home. The court granted the Trust the right to repossess the room and awarded costs against the patient.

These are depressing stories; while a much-needed bed is being occupied by someone who does not need it, the incumbent plainly wants very much to remain where they are. That in itself prompts sympathy for the patient's plight.

Nevertheless, these cases reinforce the fact that no patient is entitled to occupy a bed if they do not need clinical care requiring continuing hospital admission. We need to ensure that all options are explored for patients in this unenviable position. In doing so, it is highly likely that we will be able to discharge them in a manner which preserves their dignity and does not undermine clinical humanity. It will be rarely necessary to seek judgement in court, but from these cases, it appears that the media have understood the dilemma faced by hospitals.

CHAPTER 18

Consent for a Cannula

Anita Border v Lewisham & Greenwich [2015] EWCA Civ 8

In a recent judgement, the Court of Appeal reminded clinicians of the vital importance of consent.

A 64-year-old woman was lying in the resuscitation room of an emergency department in London while an Surgical House Officer (SHO) was proposing to insert a cannula into her left arm. This was necessary because she had a suspected fracture of her right humerus. The doctor was concerned that intravenous fluids and pain relief might very soon be required. Judging the injured arm to be unsuitable for cannulation, he wished instead to insert the line on the left; but Ms Border refused, explaining that she had recently undergone left mastectomy and axillary clearance. She had been forewarned by her oncologists of the risks of lymphoedema following infection of cuts in the skin of her left arm. The doctor considered alternative sites of cannulation, including the legs, but due to her general physical condition could not find a suitable vein. In what the court found to be a 'quick and silent calculation on his part', the SHO dismissed the alternative sites, and despite the patient's insistence, without her consent, the cannula was placed in the postmastectomy left arm. The cannula was not then immediately used for any purpose, as her medication was oral. Lymphoedema nevertheless ensued, causing her chronic disability.

Having heard from expert witnesses (in Accident and Emergency [A&E]) for both Ms Border and the Trust, the trial judge had concluded that the SHO had acted in a way that 'perhaps the great majority' of responsible A&E doctors would have done, and that the decision to insert the cannula was not negligent. The judge set this out in terms: '… [L]ooking at it from the standpoint of the expert evidence, it would be a brave decision for an SHO not to follow standard practice … that an IV line should, if possible, be inserted in the early stage'.

The trial judge dismissed the claim for damages for clinical negligence, but Ms Border disagreed and appealed.

The Court of Appeal found that notwithstanding the pressures and anxieties of being a patient in a resuscitation room, during this period the claimant retained her capacity to give or withhold consent. Furthermore, she gave no consent to the cannulation of her left arm and accordingly, the doctor who chose to insert it breached his duty of care to her.

Those reading the judgement might reasonably question what on earth the SHO was supposed to do in these circumstances. The Court of Appeal provided no assistance with this, although in fairness, courts only answer the questions posed to them, rather than advising generally upon the clinical dilemma that flows as a consequence of the judgement. In finding that Ms Border had capacity to make this decision, the appeal court simultaneously handed patients in her circumstances an unenviable choice, as they lay in that resuscitation bay: should such a patient take the risk of lymphoedema or just hope that she did not have to face a hypotensive crisis or intolerable pain without established vascular access?

If the clock could be turned back, the court presumably would expect that instead of cannulating without consent, the doctor would have explicitly laid out this stark choice to his patient. He should have spelt out to Ms Border that cannulation of an adult with capacity in the absence of their consent was not lawful. But equally, if a patient is considered ill enough to be lying in a resuscitation room, the immediately foreseeable risks of non-cannulation overshadow the theoretical later complications that the needle puncture might cause.

Should, despite this disclosure, the patient maintain the refusal, it would be prudent to revisit her capacity, record that transaction and seek another opinion before re-evaluating the situation. But as the court reminds us, consent is required.

CHAPTER 19

Changing Direction in Severe Anorexia

*Betsi Cadwaladr ULH Board v W [2016] EWCOP 13
and Cheshire & Wirral NHST v Z [2016] EWCOP 56*

We are accustomed to the situation where it may be better to prioritise the quality rather than the quantity of a patient's remaining life. This shift in emphasis is made only in conjunction with the patient or her family, but for the management of physical illness, this is rarely controversial.

The same cannot be said of mental illness. The state is bound by the Mental Health Act 1983 (MHA), which does not envisage palliation. For patients with anorexia nervosa, the English courts often view their interests as being best served by ensuring that their lives are sustained by insisting they are nourished. This law is explicitly and solely directed at treating disease of the mind rather than physical illness. But it has been interpreted over the last 20 years as regarding the need to nourish anorexic patients as 'ancillary' to the treatment of their mental illness; this physical need is duly provided for, compulsorily if necessary, via the MHA.

More recently, the approach of the courts is changing in the severest of cases. A 28-year-old woman, W, who had suffered anorexia for 20 years (having spent 10 of these years as an inpatient, mainly in specialist eating disorder units), had a body mass index (BMI) of 12.6. During her final 30-month admission, her weight loss continued, despite intensive support. Her clinicians supported their patient's request to be released into her family's care. The court accepted that W understood that her life was in danger, noting she was 'not overly concerned' by this prospect. Her history showed that she would only eat when she had deteriorated to the extent where she believed her death was imminent. But the court recognised that W's hospitalisation was no longer therapeutic; it had become 'a place for talking about eating; … not (a place) for eating'.

Ten months later, in front of a different judge, the case of Ms Z was considered. A 46-year-old woman whose anorexia nervosa had been diagnosed at 15 years of age, Ms Z lacked capacity to make decisions as to whether to undergo treatment for her anorexia, including whether to refuse or accept nasogastric feeding. The clinicians treating her had concluded that only three options existed. Firstly, to continue detention with forced nasogastric feeding (which would be hampered by Ms Z's tendency to pull out the tube) would be futile since she could control her swallowing to prevent its replacement. This option risked death and injury, due to the severest osteoporosis, and 'metabolic' cardiac failure. Her BMI was 9.5. An alternative was to feed her under continuous sedation, risking cardiorespiratory arrest.

The final option was to discharge Ms Z from the compulsion of the MHA 1983 and offer treatment only on a voluntary basis. The latter programme depended (only) on support and encouragement. The court noted that it was a pious hope that Ms Z could effectively manage her illness if left to her own devices. The judge was acutely aware that all of the options, taken at their best, were palliative, the latter being the 'least bad'.

In both cases, the courts allowed the patients to go home, released from compulsory feeding. In neither case could the court identify a better therapeutic option.

We have rarely seen courts acknowledge the impracticalities of compulsory treatment of patients with the most severe anorexia, let alone allow them to elect for the palliation of their choice.

The withdrawal of compulsory life preservation in the severest anorexic patients, when the burden of treatment outweighs the benefit they would accrue, entails them facing a daunting future. But these patients have now been given the same opportunity for palliative care that is already afforded to countless others suffering from physical disease.

CHAPTER 20

Be Informed; Then Disclose

Sebastian Webster v Burton Hospitals NHST [2017] EWCA Civ 62

The common law relating to information disclosure, when seeking consent prior to treatment, is largely founded on cases about a poor neurological outcome. This is no coincidence, since patients who suffer neurological damage during treatment often, as a consequence, need lifelong support. This support needs to be paid for, and it is for this reason, that obstetric and neurosurgical cases are brought to court. A recent case concerned a young man called Sebastian Webster. He suffered perinatal ischaemia, and now has cerebral palsy, entailing profound physical and cognitive impairment.

During his prenatal life, he was noted both to be small for gestational age (SGA) and surrounded by too much amniotic fluid. At the time of his birth, in 2003, there was emerging evidence that the combination of polyhydramnios and signs of fetal intrauterine growth restriction was indicative of, among other things, increased perinatal mortality. The High Court found that this evidence was based (in 2003) on an 'extremely small' statistical base, which would not at that stage have been reflected in official or academic guidance about the timing of delivery. The court also found that there was a body of reasonable obstetricians who would not, on the basis of the emerging evidence, have been deflected from their normal practice of awaiting a natural delivery. There were theoretical benefits for mother and baby in this conservative approach of waiting until the 42nd week to achieve a more satisfactory labour. Sebastian's obstetrician favoured the expectant approach and disclosed to his mother neither the evidence of increased perinatal death in a fetus who is SGA with polyhydramnios nor the option of induction on her due date.

It should be noted that the obstetrician told the court that he understood the issue raised by the combination of SGA and polyhydramnios. The court found that whatever he understood about the combination of these signs as indicative of possible problems, such an understanding did not extend to him believing that management of the pregnancy should have been affected by it. It also found that faced with the SGA and polyhydramnios, he should have informed himself about the significance of this combination. This information would have included the increased risk of perinatal mortality.

Once in possession of this information, the Court of Appeal found that he should then have told Sebastian's mother '... that there was an emerging but recent and incomplete material showing increased risks of delaying labour in cases with this combination of features'. The court also found that if she had been told this, the mother would have requested induction on her due date. Both parties agreed that if she had been induced on her due date, her son's injuries would have been avoided.

We have known for many years that clinicians must disclose to patients alternatives to the treatment they propose. But this story reminds us that when clinicians are faced with circumstances that they consider unusual, they are expected to familiarise themselves with the evidence attached to these circumstances. If the evidence indicates a previously unrecognised risk, it should be incorporated in the disclosure to the patient who is faced with a decision. The disclosure of this 'new' risk can be tempered by the acknowledgment that the evidence base is sparse, along the lines suggested by the court. This is by no means support for the contention that a patient can demand specific treatment from the individual doctor. In this example, if the mother, on hearing the disclosure, insisted on immediate delivery, then her obstetrician would have been perfectly entitled to decline, since in good faith he attached no importance to the combination of signs. But if he declined, he should have arranged a second opinion on the same day.

CHAPTER 21

Withdrawing Treatment in a Young Man

The Acute Trust v R [2016] EWCOP 60

The case of R, a 40-year-old man, was recently heard in the Court of Protection. Three years prior to the hearing, magnetic resonance imaging (MRI) revealed his incurable but asymptomatic brain tumour. At the time of radiological diagnosis, the tumour was considered to be low grade and non-aggressive; the clinicians had opted for an expectant approach. The patient acknowledged his diagnosis and agreed to the management.

It had been difficult to persuade him to comply with straightforward clinical appointments, and he had a tendency to behave in a hostile, threatening fashion. Two years later, a further MRI revealed unexpected rapid growth, despite a persistent lack of symptoms. The court was told that appropriately treated, his prognosis for survival could vary from 12 months to 10 years, depending on the histology, but the tumour remained incurable. By this stage, R was inconsistent as to whether he had a tumour, on some occasions altogether denying its existence. R's doctors were unanimous that he now lacked capacity to decide whether to consent for active treatment, which would consist of surgery, radiotherapy and chemotherapy.

It was for this reason that the Court of Protection was involved, since R's doctors sought a declaration that it was in his best interests not to undergo treatment for the brain tumour, but rather for him to be provided with only symptomatic care. When the legitimacy of serious medical treatment in incapacitated patients is uncertain, the Court of Protection must usually be consulted.

At first glance, it seems highly unusual to propose that life-prolonging treatment would not be in the best interests of an active 40-year-old man, irrespective of his lack of capacity. It is commonplace to perform amputations and other severe treatment on incapacitated patients whose age is much greater and prognosis much poorer than R's.

R's co-morbidity was chronic paranoid schizophrenia; he had delusional ideas including the belief that he was being interfered with by others.

The court was told of the side effects of surgical resection and that the postoperative use of dexamethasone would be hazardous, due to the risk of precipitating psychosis. Restraint and detention would be required perioperatively (although foreseeable for any incapacitated patient). R's anticipated non-compliance with the full course of radiotherapy was emphasised, linked to the risk that premature discontinuation of this treatment could paradoxically promote tumour growth. The onerous nature of chemotherapy was cited, and R's psychiatrist predicted that all three modalities of treatment would distress his patient. In particular, to force upon R compulsory treatment for which he did not understand the need would not only affront him but would lead him to resist, worsening his mental illness.

The Official Solicitor (a lawyer instructed by the court to represent R) submitted that the decision was difficult due to R's young age; it was possible that treatment would afford him a considerably longer life than if the declaration not to treat was made. He felt that if surgery alone had been required to prolong life substantially, then the risks and associated distress would be outweighed by the benefit. But taking into account the physical and mental injury and distress that the adjuvants would entail, the balance shifted, and these harms were not justified by the ultimate outcome.

In putting himself in R's position, the judge considered it was 'highly likely that he would not choose to have surgery'. With regard to all the circumstances, in particular R's probable non-cooperation and the severe effects of treatment on his mental health, the judge concluded that in the widest sense, it was in R's best interests not to receive the definitive treatment and instead to have only symptomatic palliative care.

This declaration can be seen as humane, sparing the patient abject distress that would only be recompensed by an uncertain quantity and quality of life. It is a miserable truth that his mental illness provided a formidable co-morbidity, effectively precluding life-prolonging adjuvant care. Declaring that active treatment was not in R's best interests must have been an unenviable task.

CHAPTER 22

The Value of Going to Court

NHST v HN [2016] EWCOP 43

Going to court is not an appetising prospect. But a recent case neatly illustrates how useful (and for the patient, beneficial) this can be.

In the autumn of 2016 HN, a woman in her fifties, suffering mental illness, sustained severe shoulder injuries (including a humeral shaft fracture) during an apparent suicide attempt. She refused most treatment that was offered for her injury. Some superficial injuries were healing, but several weeks later her fractured humerus rode up, presumably due to muscle spasm, and protruded through the skin. At this time, the patient was also detained under the Mental Health Act 1983 (MHA).

Her surgeon was concerned about sepsis, wishing to explore and debride the wound, with a view to future reconstruction. Meeting implacable opposition from the patient when proposing this surgery, the surgeon and anaesthetist assessed her capacity, explaining what they wanted to do and why, and the risks of both operation and non-operative management. The surgeon found that HN could understand and retain the relevant information, but could not use and weigh it to make a decision as to whether she should consent. She did not engage in discussion and gave no reason for her consistent refusal of treatment. Other clinicians were in agreement with surgery, as was HN's sole distant relative.

In this situation, the hospital was unable to rely on the MHA, since this provides authority only for compulsory treatment of diseases of the mind but no authority to treat HN's physical plight. In slightly unusual circumstances, the patient was detained for treatment of her mental illness in the same hospital as the proposed operation would be performed, making it legally impossible to treat her under the Mental Capacity Act 2005 (MCA). Usually, such patients are *transferred* from a mental hospital to an acute trust (under what is known as s17 leave) for surgery. Once in the acute hospital, the s17 legitimises compulsory mental treatment. The MCA can then be employed to authorise physical treatment if the patient lacks capacity, as well as any necessary deprivation of liberty. For these reasons, among others, the hospital sought a declaration from the court that compulsory treatment of HN's wound was lawful.

With the clinician and family member in agreement that wound exploration was in HN's best interests, the hospital made an urgent out-of-hours application to the Court of Protection on a Friday evening, proposing to operate 'no later than the (Saturday) morning'. The hospital told the court that failure to deal with the current situation might lead to a variant of forequarter amputation or fulminant sepsis.

The court found, during a telephone hearing, that it was in the patient's best interests to have this relatively minor operation in order to prevent more serious harm, and it authorised the surgery. But it reminded the clinicians that should further surgery be required in due course, a separate application should be made.

It was subsequently confirmed that the surgery took place as planned, with the patient going to theatre without objection, restraint or sedation. Nonetheless, microbiology from intraoperative samples confirmed that bony infection was already established.

This case was always destined for court because of the legal difficulties related to operating on a 'sectioned' patient in a hospital where she was already detained for treatment of her underlying mental illness.

But the wider point is that the courts provide much, much more than a forum for litigation for alleged substandard medical care. Crucially, the High Court acts as a non-partisan arbiter for disputes as to where a patient's best interests lie. While clinicians may be certain that intervention is appropriate, the unbefriended incapacitated patient has no voice with which to challenge this 'certainty'. In these circumstances, when serious compulsory medical treatment of an incapacitated adult is an issue, it is right to seek independent judicial scrutiny of the decision as to the patient's best interests.

CHAPTER 23

Articulating Best Interests

Salford Royal NHSFT v P & Q [2017] EWCOP 23

We are all well aware that adults with capacity make their own treatment decisions. There is no call to determine the best interests of such patients, since they can (by definition) decide these matters for themselves. Accordingly, their 'best interests' are never explored. Naturally, clinicians will on occasion disagree with a capacitous patient's decision, and they are at liberty to try and persuade the patient to change his or her mind, but the patient with capacity has the last word. This is starkly exemplified by the adult with capacity who chooses to refuse the blood that would otherwise have saved his life, or the woman with capacity who refuses the caesarean section that alone would allow her child to be born alive.

But for those who lack capacity to make decisions relating to their treatment, clinicians have become accustomed to acting in the patient's best interests. Meetings devoted to this subject are a ubiquitous daily occurrence in hospitals across the country. Again, we are all well aware of the general principles standing behind 'best interests'; the incapacitated patient's welfare must be scrutinised in its widest terms not simply in the sense of medical but also social and psychological interests. This will involve consideration of the proposed medical treatment, the prospects of success and the likely outcome. That is all very well; how should we achieve this?

A case decided in October 2017 provided us with clear, specific guidance concerning Mrs P, who was 72 years old when she suffered the intracranial bleed that left her in a minimally conscious state. It was agreed that there was no prospect of her regaining the capacity to make decisions relating to her health; it was speculated that her potential life expectancy was in the region of 3–5 years. Nonetheless, she was otherwise relatively healthy and the hospital wished to insert a gastrostomy for hydration and nourishment. She would not tolerate a nasogastric tube, the presence (and frequent replacement) of which distressed her. Mrs P's daughters disagreed with this proposal, explaining that their mother had previously expressed a wish not to be kept alive if severely handicapped, especially if her mental function were severely affected.

Because of this disagreement, the court was approached, the hospital seeking a declaration that the proposed treatment was lawful. The judgement was centred on the notion that when considering best interests, decision-makers must try to put themselves in the place of the individual patient and ask what her attitude to the proposed treatment is likely to be. And they must consult those who befriend or look after the patient, in particular to obtain a view on what her attitude to the treatment might be. Factors that should be taken into account would include the views of those who had a close relationship with the patient when she had capacity and the impact of the patient's fate on those who were closest to her.

The court nevertheless made it crystal clear that what the patient would have done in the circumstances (if their capacity had been preserved) would not automatically be regarded as to be in her best interests. While courts (and clinical decision-makers) will strive to recognise and comply with what the patient is likely to have wanted, acting in her best interests remains the para-mount objective.

As an example: if a patient's history reveals a series of damaging lifestyle decisions, and it is concluded that she would, if she could, continue this life-style, the decision-maker would likely conclude that allowing the patient to sustain further damage would be contrary to her best interests.

Equally, in a patient who would have wished to persist with hourly repeated episodes of cardiopulmonary resuscitation despite being told correctly that there was no prospect of a sustainable cardiac rhythm, those subsequently making decisions on his behalf might well conclude that the burden of pain and loss of dignity outweighed the benefit and that contrary to his capacitious wish, his best interests lay in cessation of resuscitation.

It was therefore by no means clear at the start of the case that the court would regard Mrs P's expressed wish for non-treatment as compatible with her best interests.

Hearing all the evidence, the judge concluded that for Mrs P, her high level of dependency on clinical services combined with her minimal awareness would be a 'travesty' of life; and that she was entitled to her view. The hearing (and the inquiries necessitated by it) allowed her voice to be heard. The hospital's application was refused.

CHAPTER 24

Loyal Friends

Sheffield Teaching Hospitals v TH & TR [2014] EWCOP 4

Every adult in England has the opportunity to anticipate their future incapacity, and make efforts to influence, among other things, the medical treatment they receive. Perhaps the most adaptable mechanism is to appoint a Lasting Power of Attorney, armed with the authority to make certain treatment decisions, which can include the decision to refuse life-prolonging treatment. Less effective is the provision of an Advance Decision (AD) to refuse treatment, since it is very difficult to anticipate the details of one's eventual deterioration. Faced with an AD that does not closely correspond to your precise clinical circumstances, most clinicians will err on the side of caution, particularly when life is at stake. Under these circumstances, your capacitious plea from long ago not to be resuscitated may fail as the doctor gives you the 'benefit of the doubt', and defibrillates. This is an act of good faith, but not in accord with what you had hoped for.

There are less legalistic options. Some citizens set out their wishes and feelings in an advance statement, with no lawyer in sight; this can be on paper or online, with the aspiration that it may one day join the much vaunted electronic record. Since advance statements are essentially a narrative of one's wishes, beliefs and feelings, they can in theory be very powerful. Unencumbered by the legal requirement of Lasting Powers of Attorney and ADs anything the advance statement loses in legal force it gains as a more tangible, understandable, human plea for limiting future treatment.

And these mechanisms always do that; patients are (of course) perfectly entitled to plead for a particular treatment, but they have no right to demand a therapy in the National Health Service which doctors do not consider to be in their best interests.

The following case demonstrates the power of narrative, albeit one constructed by the patient's friends. TH was a 52-year-old man at the most severe position on the spectrum of a minimally conscious state. His case was being heard in a court whose duty it was to decide whether his nutrition and hydration should be withdrawn. Although the hearing was going to be adjourned for the court later to hear additional medical evidence, the court took the opportunity to hear from the patient's friends, in relation to any relevant feelings or wishes he might have expressed.

TH's friends transported his character and personality into the courtroom, communicating his words and wishes, and also, but entirely differently, his feelings. It was clear to the court from the outset of evidence that TH had never had a conversation with his friends that anticipated his current plight, so that the legal requirements of an AD could not be met. But the power of the narrative was not diminished by its lack of legal weight. No one 'portrayed TH as a hero', beset as he was by alcohol dependency and past demons. He was profoundly distrustful of the State and all its works. While still living in great difficulty at home, TH had refused to allow care workers to bathe him, and asked his ex-wife to help him. Despite the breakdown of their marriage, she did so, since she knew he could not face the indignity of being bathed by strangers.

What was clear was TH's loathing of hospitals, from which he would remove himself at the earliest opportunity, notwithstanding the resultant damage to all aspects of his health. The court found that in many 'oblique and tangential ways', TH had over many years communicated his views to his friends in an uncompromising and blunt fashion, eradicating any lingering doubt that he would wish to continue his life in his present circumstances. He would, if he could, refuse life-sustaining treatment. The judge was certain that TH would want to leave hospital and end his days quietly and with dignity at home with his friends.

The court's eventual judgement, following adjournment, has not been reported in the intervening 3 years. We are left to speculate whether TH's wishes were realised, but are in no doubt as to the loyalty of his friends.

CHAPTER 25

Apply to Court?

NHST v Y & Y [2017] EWHC 2866 QB

In clinical practice, decisions relating to adults who lack capacity are ubiquitous, both in relation to the need for new treatment, and concerning current management that is no longer in the best interests of the patient. Some of these decisions can only be taken by a court. For example, the performance of an elective non-therapeutic sterilisation on an incapacitated adult is considered such an affront to that person's human right (to a family life) that in the United Kingdom, surgeons are not permitted to perform this operation without first seeking a court's permission.

Since the case of Tony Bland, a survivor of the Hillsborough Stadium disaster, the question of whether a patient who is in a persistent vegetative state can have their clinically assisted nutrition and hydration (CANH) withdrawn has also (as a matter of practice) been referred to court.

It should be clearly understood that neither non-therapeutic sterilisation nor withholding CANH are inherently unlawful activities; both could be legitimised by the consent of an adult with capacity. It is only in cases where the patient lacks capacity that an application to a court is required. In neither of the previous examples is the question for the court whether the activity is lawful. The court has no power to render something lawful that without the court's sanction would be unlawful. Rather, the question for the court is whether the non-therapeutic sterilisation, or the withdrawal of CANH, is in the best interests of the incapacitated patient.

Two cases have caused courts to consider whether, when there is no disagreement about the decision to withdraw CANH, referral to the court is any longer required. In *Re M*, all those concerned with a woman (who was in a minimally conscious state as a result of Huntingdon's disease) felt that her CANH should be withdrawn, but nevertheless felt that an 'external' decision should be taken. Since there was no dispute between clinicians and the family as to the best interests of the patient, the judge decided that based on the facts of Mrs M's case, there was no legal requirement for the decision to withdraw CANH to be taken by the court. In the report of Mrs M's case, the (1993)

Bland judgement* was cited, one of the judges noting that '... at least for the time being and until a body of experience and practice had been built up ... applications in every case as a matter of routine should be made'. The decision in Mrs M's case may reflect the contemporary court's view that in 2017, this body of experience is now established.

In the case of Mr Y, a 52-year-old investment banker who suffered severe brain damage after a 10-minute cardiac standstill secondary to occlusive coronary artery disease; the clinical team and his family agreed that it was not in his best interest to continue to receive treatment. Neurological experts agreed that he had no awareness of self or his environment, and that it was 'highly improbable' that he would regain consciousness.

The Trust looking after Mr Y was supported by his wife in seeking a declaration that there was no mandatory requirement to seek consent from a court to withdraw CANH in circumstances when there is no dispute between clinicians and family as to the incapacitated patient's best interests.

The Official Solicitor appointed to represent Mr Y submitted that there was a common law obligation to ensure that Mr Y's right to life was not infringed, and to provide independent scrutiny of the decision.

The High Court found that the previous decided cases in the common law did not establish a principle that all instances concerning the proposed withdrawal of CANH from a person who lacks capacity must be sanctioned by a court. Where clinicians have followed the Mental Capacity Act 2005 and good medical practice, and there is no dispute with the patient's family, or anyone else interested in his welfare, there is no requirement to bring the matter before a court.

Although this judgement continues a recent trend, we must await the view of the Supreme Court; the High Court took steps to launch and expedite the appeal process.

If the Supreme Court agrees to consider the case, the circumstances in which decisions to withdraw CANH (and other life-sustaining treatments) should be

---

* Airedale NHST v Bland [1993] AC 789.LE4

brought to the court will be reviewed. This may significantly change the law that governs decision-making for incapacitated patients.

Such a change would have a tangible influence on how cases are resolved when clinicians and families are in agreement as to where the patient's best interests lie.

Postscript: Please see case in Chapter 61.

CHAPTER 26

Disclosing the Miniscule Risk When Seeking Consent

Mrs A v East Kent Hospitals University NHSFT [2015] EWHC 1038 QB
Rogers v Whittaker [1992] 109 ALR 625 (Aust.HC)

The foreseeable risks associated with clinical practice seem innumerable, and when seeking a patient's consent for treatment, we are faced daily with the prospect of trying to identify what we will and will not disclose. An obvious criterion for making this judgement is the frequency with which the risk occurs. Historically, clinicians, most notably surgeons, chose an arbitrary number ... perhaps 1% or 0.1% frequency of the risk crystallising ... below which they would not disclose the risk when seeking a patient's consent. At least 30 years ago, the common law guided us away from this practice; requiring us to disclose risks that would be seen as significant to the reasonable person in the position of the patient we are dealing with, providing no comment as to what magnitude of risk that reasonable person might regard as significant.

In the Supreme Court's recent case of *Montgomery**, that viewpoint was reiterated; the doctor must make the patient aware of any material risks. And that the test of materiality is (*i*) whether in the circumstances of the particular case, a reasonable person in the patient's position would be likely to attach significance to the risk, or (*ii*) the doctor should be reasonably aware that the particular patient in front of them would be likely to attach significance to it.

The clinical duty is of 'reasonable care'. This indicates that no absolute duty is involved, and for that reason, there is no requirement to disclose all risks. Material risks must however be disclosed. This is all very well, but does the court give illustrations as to the relevance of frequency?

In a 2015 decision, the High Court considered the case of Mrs A who conceived with the aid of in vitro fertilisation, and whose third-trimester ultrasound scans revealed poor fetal growth. Following full-term delivery, it

---

* Montgomery v Lanarkshire Health Board [2015] UKSC 11

became obvious that the baby was severely disabled as a result of a balanced 4:11 chromosomal translocation. Mrs A claimed that if she had known of the risk of chromosome anomaly antenatally she would have undergone amniocentesis, and on confirming the presence of this translocation, would have terminated her pregnancy.

The court was told that the actuarial antenatal risk of poor fetal growth in this baby's case being due to a chromosomal anomaly was on the order of 0.1%.

The court found that a reasonable person in Mrs A's position would consider a risk of 0.1% as being negligible, theoretical or background, and would not have attached significance to it. Nonetheless, the court indicated that if the risk had been on the order of 1%–3%, it would have regarded this a risk that a reasonable person would have attached significance to, and thus regarded as material. In addition, the court noted that in her evidence, Mrs A attached no significance to the fact that (during her pregnancy) she ran a 1:1750 risk that she could be carrying a baby with Down syndrome. She refused investigations to exclude this diagnosis, since she did not want to endanger her fetus by premature delivery. The court found that in the same way, Mrs A herself would not have considered a risk of 0.1% significant.

The role of the particular patient's attitude to a risk in different circumstances is demonstrated by the Australian case of Maree Whittaker. She had suffered a penetrating injury to her eyeball as a child, and considered herself disfigured by the subsequent appearance. Forty years later, she sought cosmetic surgery for the deformed globe. She was adamant that she would not have surgery if it entailed risk to her healthy contralateral eye, since she feared blindness. Assured there was none, she underwent surgery and suffered sympathetic ophthalmia, where the sight of her healthy eye was severely damaged. The risk of sympathetic ophthalmia was 1:14,000, a miniscule risk. But the court held that this particular patient attached significance to the risk of blindness that transpired in her non-operated eye, and should have had this risk disclosed to her, irrespective of its rarity. Her case was decided in 1992, and remains good law.

It can be seen that 'materiality' is slowly taking shape. The courts, on behalf of the reasonable person in the patient's position, indicate that risks of 1%–3% would be regarded as material, but 0.1% risks are not. But when considering the particular patient in the context of the facts of her case, a 1:14,000 risk may be highly significant and thus found to be material, and necessary to disclose. If a patient voices fears about the possibility of a particular risk, irrespective of its frequency, it seems natural to disclose its existence.

Mrs A gives no authority for the proposition that background, negligible or theoretical risks cannot be material. As *Whittaker* shows us, they can be. Such 'miniscule' risks may be engaged as material risks in elective, non-therapeutic or cosmetic procedures where the option of no treatment or conservative non-surgical treatment is available. Do not discount the possibility that for a particular patient, even miniscule risks may need to be disclosed to ensure valid consent.

CHAPTER 27

Obtaining Consent

Lisa Thefaut v Francis Johnston [2017] EWHC 497 QB

A recent judgement explores the practicalities of obtaining valid consent for surgery, exposing some difficulties in that process. The case related to a woman (Mrs T) presenting with leg pain caused by the prolapse of an L4/L5 intervertebral disc. It was agreed that expectant management would have probably resulted in resolution of her symptoms, but that this resolution could have been accelerated by discectomy. Regrettably, after competently performed surgery, Mrs T nonetheless experienced disabling leg pain, arguably consistent with injury to the L5 nerve root. She also experiences altered sensation which is said to be consistent with S2 and S3 nerve injuries.

The court found that the surgeon overstated the likelihood that she would enjoy a symptomatic improvement as the result of surgery. In addition, the court found that the surgeon emphasised an eradication of pain rather than acknowledging to the patient that amelioration would have been a more realistic expectation. The option of having no surgery was in Mrs T's case a very important alternative to surgical intervention, and the court accepted that she was aware of this from conversations with her surgeon. By contrast, the detailed written information was found to be unreasonable. The letter describing the potential complications of the forthcoming operation risked confusing the patient that the expectant approach was of no real significance, or that it had been superseded by the requirement for an operation as the only option.

It was agreed that the surgeon did not advise Mrs T of the inherent risk (up to 5%) that any procedure could exacerbate her condition; despite disclosing less frequently occurring risks. Again, omission of this disclosure was found to be highly relevant when compared or contrasted with the alternative of no operation, with the likelihood of gradually receding pain and ultimately spontaneous recovery within 12 months.

The court noted that the routine meeting between Mrs T and her surgeon on the day of operation allowed both to ensure that they remained committed to its performance.

By contrast, in an aside not relevant to Mrs T's claim, the court asserted generally that the routine meeting between patient and surgeon on the day of the operation is '... neither the place nor the occasion for a surgeon for the first time to explain to a patient undergoing elective surgery the risks and benefits'. This represents rare High Court advice to clinicians who are considering new disclosures on the day of surgery. The reasoning behind that advice was based on the judicial observation that 'on the very cusp of the procedure', both the surgeon and patient are distracted. The surgeon by pressure of time, and the patient by their psychological commitment to proceed: 'There is a mutual momentum towards (elective) surgery which it is hard to halt; (there is) no adequate time and space for a free choice and sensible dialogue to take place'.

The court found that objectively, the reasonable patient in Mrs T's position would (following the necessary disclosure) have either rejected surgery or sought a second opinion. Subjectively, taking her evidence into account, the court concluded the same thing. Similarly, if Mrs T had sought a second opinion, the reasonable advice that she would have obtained would have led her to refuse surgery. The court also explored the extent to which subjective factors relating to the patient that the surgeon is dealing with are relevant. The starting position is the test in *Montgomery**; whether, '...in the circumstances of the particular case, a reasonable person in the patient's position would be likely to attach significance to the risk'. This combines the objective standard of the reasonable patient with the subjectivity of the person in the particular case. The judge identified characteristics which may not be self-evident in a clinic, such as a patient's ability to deal with pain, or their need to continue employment, or the effects of a coincidental crisis such as divorce or bereavement, and in addition, the implications for mobility and treasured sports and hobbies. To this could be added difficulties with their dependent children's education or impending homelessness or prosecution. Any of these may render a normally resolute person temporarily more fragile and, in turn, less willing to run a risk.

The great difficulty for clinicians is how they might enable the patient to scrutinise these subjective factors during their decision-making for surgery, rather than only consider them following surgical misadventure, later reflecting that on the basis of their situation, they would not have run the risk in the first place. While these intensely personal aspects of a patient's life remain unknown to the surgeon, it would seem unjust to expect them to appreciate the ramifications that foreseeable risks of surgery may have for the patient. It remains to be seen how far the English courts will go in allowing claimants to dress the reasonable person in their particular clothes.

---

* Montgomery v Lanarkshire Health Board [2015] UKSC 11

CHAPTER 28

Deprivation of Liberty:
The Story So Far

P v Cheshire West & Chester Council & Ors [2014] UKSC 19
R (Ferreira) v HM Senior Coroner for Inner South
London & Ors [2017] EWCA Civ 31

The 2014 judgement in 'Cheshire West' caused clinical consternation. The case concerned, among others, P, a 37-year-old man with Down syndrome and cerebral palsy. He lacked capacity to make any decision in relation to his living arrangements. He required 24-hour care, provided in a local authority bungalow which he shared with two other residents, and constant staff supervision. He was provided weekly with 98 hours additional one-to-one support to allow him to leave the house whenever he chose, visiting a day centre or hydrotherapy each weekday. He also was accompanied to clubs, pubs and shops, with or without a wheelchair, dependent on distance. With prompting and help he could deal with eating, personal hygiene and continence. For the latter he wore pads, together with a 'body suit' to prevent him from ripping his pads and putting pieces in his mouth. He had other challenging behaviours for which intervention was required. The question for the court was whether these residential arrangements constituted a deprivation of liberty imposed by the state. If so, it would be necessary for the state to put in place mechanisms whereby the deprivation was authorised and controlled, to avoid disproportionate or unnecessary violations of P's human right to liberty.

The Supreme Court concluded that because he lacked capacity (and could therefore not consent), was under continuous (state) supervision and control and not free to leave, he was deprived of his liberty. This Lady Hale christened 'the acid test'. Although the first and last paragraphs of the leading judgement made clear that its focus was on living arrangements for incapacitated persons, the effect on acute hospitals has been profound, since many patients lie within acute care areas manifestly incapacitated (on ventilators, for instance) and certainly 'under continuous supervision & control, not free to leave'. For several years, with various degrees of success, acute medical facilities in the United Kingdom tried to ensure that patients whose liberty was genuinely threatened were not 'lost' in the tumult of applications, many taking 20–30 weeks to be responded to, many months after the patient, restored, had gone home.

Mercifully, a judgement in 2017 brought this clinical crisis to a close. The case concerned Maria Ferreira, a 45-year-old woman with Down syndrome, who presented to an intensive care unit with pneumonia and pericarditis. She was sedated, intubated and under constant observation. Ultimately, Ms Ferreira died in intensive care; the question for the coroner was whether she was in 'state detention' at the time: were her Article 5 rights to liberty infringed (and could the Deprivation of Liberty Safeguards [DOLS] have been invoked?).

The Court of Appeal did not find that her presence in the intensive care, despite her lacking capacity and meeting the acid test, equated to a deprivation of liberty. 'The root cause of any loss of liberty (suffered by Ms Ferreira) lay in restrictions arising from her physical infirmities and the treatment which she received … *Cheshire West* was distinguishable because it was directed to living arrangements for persons of unsound mind. It provided no guidance to the context of urgent or intensive care treatment in hospital … where the true cause of the patient not being free to leave was their illness rather than the consequence of state action'.

Happily, many patients respond to treatment, and their physical condition improves. The point may be reached where the patient has recovered sufficiently whereby they would be able to leave hospital. But due to incapacity many are under complete supervision and control, not free to leave while awaiting the availability of residential care in the community. In this situation, the 'acid test' is passed, and authority must be sought for their deprivation of liberty.

In June 2017, the Supreme Court refused permission for this judgement to be further appealed, thus the Court of Appeal's decision in *Ferreira* is considered authoritative and binding. In the meantime, it had become apparent that the DOLS process required urgent review, and this prompted the Law Commission and then Parliament to act. The result was the creation of statutory 'Liberty Protection Safeguards', eagerly awaited in 2020. Accompanied by a new Code of Practice, these will prescribe management for people of 16 years and over who lack capacity, and whose liberty is at risk.

CHAPTER 29

Falling from Hospital Property

Spearman v Royal United Bath Hospitals [2017] EWHC 3027 QB

Hospitals have a duty to prevent incapacitated patients from hurting them-selves. In 2011, James Spearman, a 47-year-old man lacking capacity was briefly left unattended in an emergency department. He tried to leave. Passing through an unsecured door he ascended five flights of stairs onto a flat roof. Piling up the outdoor furniture that he found there, he climbed over an incurving 1.4-metre barrier. At around 22.15, in the darkness, James fell to the courtyard below.

He had developed type 1 diabetes at the age of 11 years, and then in 1987 suf-fered a traumatic brain injury when in his early twenties. This injury required many months of rehabilitation; his family explained that as a result 'James detests hospitals'. The brain injury transformed him from an insurance broker to a person who lived a much-restricted life, but with a significant personality change. At times, he had very limited self-awareness and empathy with those surrounding him. This paradox of independence while lacking awareness is illustrated by the fact that by 1990, he was able to fly to a shooting trip in Scotland, but was arrested in Terminal 1 Heathrow as he returned, since he chose to clean his shotgun while waiting to go through border control. This episode illustrates how Mr Spearman could fix upon an objective that he was trying to achieve while remaining oblivious to risks that this would entail.

On the night of his fall from the roof, James had been admitted with confu-sion after a hypoglycaemic episode. Following his fall into the courtyard, he can no longer live independently, needing assistance with all aspects of daily living.

Perhaps because of James' new and permanent utter dependency, a claim against the hospital was made by his family. The court found that nowhere on the route that he had taken to the roof were there signs that access was unauthorised; the doors were unlocked. The court found that the hospital should have provided direct nursing supervision of this confused patient, and restricted his movements by locking doors. The 'lowest common denominator' of the hospital's duty was to take reasonable steps to provide for the safety of vulnerable patients with a mental disorder. Failure to control access to the flat roof was singled out by the judge as a reasonably foreseeable cause of an otherwise avoidable accident.

The defending hospital asked the court to consider whether Mr Spearman had contributed to the harm that he suffered by leaving the emergency department, and by failing to inform the staff that he was going to leave, or that he wanted to hurt himself. The judge made it crystal clear that he could not attribute blame to the patient on these grounds, any more than one would blame a young child for running out into the road. He found that neither this theoretical child, nor the patient in question could appreciate the danger they put themselves into. 'Otherwise, that would be to penalise a person for being ill or of unsound mind, and the law does not do that'.

This judgement suggests that our duty to ensure that vulnerable patients do not come to harm on hospital premises may extend to a need to control and supervise more generally the movement of patients in areas to which they have access. If the judge's decision is followed by higher courts, this will have a significant effect on our practice. Either way, it can hardly be criticised on the grounds of common sense.

CHAPTER 30

Gross Negligence Manslaughter: Perhaps Better, 'Betrayal of Trust'?

Bawa-Garba v GMC & Ors [2018] EWCA Civ 1879
(Betrayal of Trust in Medical Manslaughter. Journal
of Criminal Law 2019 83 (6) 489–502)

If a clinician is suspected by the police of gross negligence manslaughter the point will be reached where, in England and Wales, the Crown Prosecution Service (CPS) must make a decision as to whether the clinician should be charged with this crime. If charged, the accused will stand trial, unless they plead guilty. One of the key factors in making this decision is whether there is 'a realistic prospect of conviction', in other words, whether the court is more likely than not to convict. This begs the question whether (assuming the allegations are proven in trial) the jury will find the defendant guilty. To predict this, it is important to consider what guidance the judge will give the jury with respect to what 'gross negligence' entails. After all, if the defendant has not been grossly negligent, then the jury must acquit.

Medical experts provide the court with an opinion as to whether care was substandard. But the issue of whether substandard care ('negligence') amounts to gross negligence is a matter for the jury alone.

In a case involving a doctor who failed to send promptly a patient to hospital, the court in *R v Bateman (1925)*[*] provided this guidance as to what gross negligence might mean:

> In explaining to juries the test which they should apply to determine whether the negligence, in the particular case, amounted or did not amount to a crime, the judges have used many epithets, such as 'culpable', 'criminal', 'gross', 'wicked', 'clear', 'complete'. But whatever epithet be used and whether an epithet be used or not, in order to establish criminal liability the facts must be such that, in the opinion of the jury ... the negligence of the accused went beyond a mere

---

[*] R v Bateman (1925) 94 LJKB 791

matter of compensation between subjects and showed such disregard for the life and safety of others as to amount to a crime against the state and conduct deserving punishment.

In a more recent case, involving failure to recognise that an anaesthetic ventilation circuit was disconnected for 4 minutes, *R v Adomako (1993)** the court (accepting the rubric from *Bateman*) set out a circumstantial analysis of what could constitute gross negligence:

• Indifference to an obvious risk of injury to health
• Actual foresight of the risk coupled with the determination nevertheless to run it
• Actual foresight of the risk together with an intention to avoid it but involving such a high degree of negligence in the attempted avoidance as the jury considered justified conviction
• Inattention or failure to advert to a serious risk going beyond mere inadvertence in respect of an important matter which the defendant's duty demanded he should address

In the case of Dr Bawa-Garba, initially convicted for this crime after the death of a child, the judicial epithet used to describe to the jury the threshold for gross negligence was whether her failings were 'truly exceptionally bad', or not. It is unknown whether members of this jury clearly understood the question they were required to answer.

Does the guidance in *Bateman* and *Adomako* properly equip a jury to be able to recognise 'gross negligence'? The fact that judges continue to use their own epithets may indicate otherwise, if they feel that in 2018, nearly 100 years after *Bateman*, yet further definition for the jury is called for. If, in turn, the CPS is also unable clearly to define the elements of this offence, how can they be certain that they are using the charging threshold consistently? Perhaps a more coherent and reproducible approach to making the decision to charge doctors with gross negligence manslaughter is required.

The legal basis for prosecution and conviction for gross negligence manslaughter has arguably failed to provide prosecutors, judges and juries with sufficient certainty as to what constitutes the offence in the nineteenth or twentieth centuries. Founding the charge on the basis of a betrayal of trust between the patient and doctor may represent a concept that a jury can recognise and empathise with. If a jury can understand a binary decision of

_____

* R v Adomako [1993] 4 All ER 935

betrayal versus non-betrayal, then the judge's task of direction will be simplified, less ambiguous, providing certainty. At the same time, the CPS may find it easier to identify the rare cases of betrayal of trust that merit prosecution.

Postscript: Dr Bawa-Garba's leave to appeal her conviction was refused by the Court of Appeal on 29 November 2016. Nevertheless, an appeal of her erasure from the Medical Register was allowed in 2018, restoring her registration.

CHAPTER 31

Interpretation

Nilujan Rajatheepan v Barking, Havering & Redbridge
NHSFT [2018] EWHC 716 (QB)

A 21-year-old Sri Lankan woman had given birth to her first baby on the 16th of July. At that time, she spoke very few words of English; the antenatal records revealed at booking that she spoke Tamil, and an interpreter was required. As the clinics progressed at two monthly intervals, it was repeatedly noticed that she needed an interpreter.

After delivery, the mother wished to breastfeed, starting in the postnatal ward on the day after birth. She believed her baby was feeding well, although the following day he started to cry, apparently inconsolably despite repeated breastfeeds. His mother worried he was hungry, and twice called the ward staff. The mother described how on one occasion, the midwife placed the child supine and tried to pacify him, failed to do so, then returned the baby to her and departed. The mother persevered with feeding, and whenever a nurse passed by they would smile and nod at each other, but no words could be exchanged, and the mother could not communicate her increasing concerns for her crying infant.

The mother was adamant in her evidence that at no stage during her admission did the midwives explain how to breastfeed her baby, although she was taught how to change a nappy.

On Sunday the 18th of July, her husband (who spoke basic English) was asked in the evening to take his wife and baby home; the mother told the court she did not understand that she was being discharged, but remained concerned about her baby's constant crying. She asked her husband to relay to the midwives her anxieties, and to explain she had received no assistance throughout the day in resolving the infant's distress. While placing the baby in the car seat, a midwife explained it was normal for newborns to cry; this advice was repeated to family members on several occasions.

The baby went home with his parents, and he continued to cry through the night, irrespective of his mother's efforts to breastfeed. By morning, he made less effort to feed; she reasoned he had tired himself from crying. A midwife who visited him at home discovered the baby to be pale and lethargic. On admission to hospital he was hypoglycaemic, and as a result had suffered catastrophic brain injury, resulting in severely impaired physical and cognitive function. The court found, after litigation, that this was a result of the child not being fed; 12–15 hours of non-feeding were sufficient to exhaust energy reserves and result in profound hypoglycaemia, followed by irreversible cerebral injury.

The court found that the devastatingly simple cause was attributable to the baby's mother having no knowledge of how to breastfeed, and crucially, no knowledge of what to do if there was poor feeding.

The court also found that the mother's (albeit timid) attempts to engage with the midwives had been ignored. The discharge process had been conducted without interpretation facilities for the mother, and failed to give the concerns that were being raised about the baby the attention and consideration that they deserved. By repeating to the father a mantra that 'it is perfectly normal for a newborn to cry', false reassurance was given to the family, discouraging them from repeating once more the concerns already raised; ostensibly allayed.

Treating every year more patients who require language interpretation, we must be alert to the grave risks that flow from failure to communicate with our patient. No clinician can assume that apparently intuitive, instinctive acts such as feeding a baby are necessarily adequately understood by the patient. Providing elementary information may be straightforward when we share a common language with the patient. But when need be, please ensure successful interpreted communication before discharge.

CHAPTER 32

A Narrow Dispute

PW v Chelsea & Westminster Hospital NHSFT &
RW & Ors [2018] EWCA Civ 1067

Mr W, a 77-year-old man with end-stage dementia lacked capacity to make decisions about his treatment. Admitted to hospital in September 2017 with an acute illness, a nasogastric tube was passed to enable his enteral feeding. Within 2 months, he was well enough to return home, but his discharge was delayed due to a disagreement with his family. The dispute centred on whether he should go home with the nasogastric tube in place for continued provision of nourishment and hydration. On numerous occasions in the ensuing 6 months in hospital his tube was displaced and repassed, with consequential significant abrasions to his nares and radiography after each replacement. Mr W had no motor or verbal response to stimuli other than opening his eyes when his hand was pushed. The court was told that his Glasgow Coma Scale (GCS) score was 4; he suffered contractures, and had lost both his swallow capacity and any signs of hunger. He was doubly incontinent, and entirely dependent on others for his personal care.

During the ensuing court hearing to settle where Mr W's best interests lay in the dispute over nasogastric feeding at home, it was agreed that Mr W should be discharged to the care of his sons, with domiciliary clinical support. It was also agreed that insertion of a gastrostomy was not in his best interests, nor was cardiopulmonary resuscitation.

The sons meanwhile sought a declaration that Mr W should be discharged with the nasogastric tube in situ, while the Trust pleaded for a declaration that he should be allowed to go home with a plan for palliative care and oral comfort feeding, following removal of the nasogastric tube prior to discharge.

The hospital's case was that long-term nasogastric feeding of adults with dementia in the community is rare, with a paucity of evidence measuring safety and efficacy. Nasal and oesophageal trauma associated with tube insertion, together with aspiration and tube dislodgement were all commonplace and rendered home nasogastric feeding unsafe for Mr W.

The family's view differed. They felt Mr W had tolerated 8 months of feeding in hospital well, and that they could significantly reduce the risk of displacement by providing continuous care at home. Mr W's sons had received training in tube care, and they noted the acknowledged risk of aspiration *in the absence* of a tube.

Mr W's son, in evidence, reported that his father 'never wanted to go back to hospital', and had been a stoical man. At the High Court, the Trust's application was granted.

On appeal, the court noted that the High Court judge had taken careful account of evidence of Mr W's wishes, feelings, beliefs and values. She accepted that he would have wanted to be cared for at home, but not that there was dependable evidence that he would have wished to receive continuing feeding by nasogastric tube. She accepted the medical view that this was inappropriate, and that this view was consistent with National Institute for Health and Care Excellence and General Medical Council guidance. She also gave careful consideration to the risks and benefits of the different methods of feeding.

Contrary to the family's assertion that the High Court had not given enough weight to what Mr W would have wanted in these circumstances, and that the judge had overstated the risks of tube feeding at home, the Court of Appeal found no error in her decision, and upheld the Trust's application.

This case, turning as it does on the single issue of whether or not an elderly patient should go home with nasogastric tube feeding echoes a very common practical problem facing acute hospital trusts across the country. The court found that the patient's best interests had precedence over the family's (undoubtedly well-intentioned) insistence that tube feeding must continue after discharge. Demonstrating that on occasion, judicial authority is necessary to ensure that patient's welfare is given priority.

CHAPTER 33

A Right to Be Told?

Gallardo v Imperial College NHST [2017] EWHC 3147 (QB)

Mr Gallardo complained that he had not been told of his malignant diagnosis, and that a plan for following his postoperative course had not been put in place. At the age of 28 years, he had presented with what appeared to be a gastric ulcer, but proved at operation in 2001 to be a malignant gastrointestinal stromal tumour (GIST) requiring subtotal gastrectomy. His early postoperative course was complicated by acute appendicitis and two further laparotomies for sepsis and obstruction, all necessitating 6 weeks intensive and then high-dependency care.

Leaving the hospital apparently oblivious of his malignant condition, he had no follow-up clinical review or imaging, only to present 9 years later with recurrent disease.

The court hearing his claim found that he had not been told that his operation had revealed a malignancy, that he should have been told, and that follow-up arrangements should have been put in place.

This is not a surprising conclusion, and reflects the energy that all clinicians must expend to ensure that interventions are followed up according to the diagnosis that is reached. The case is nonetheless of interest because it reveals the creation of a judicial standard for clinical follow-up, which is rare and bears scrutiny.

The judge applied the familiar rules for information disclosure prior to consent for any clinical intervention (set out, as we are all well aware, in the General Medical Council's guidelines from June 2008) to information that we need to provide *following* that intervention. While you may consider that this strains the sinews of 'informed consent' to breaking point, Hughes J articulated an obligation by analogy; to provide the patient with '… a right to be informed of the outcome of treatment, the prognosis, and what the follow up care and treatment options are. Information should only be withheld in exceptional circumstances and for clear and persuasive therapeutic reasons'.

In finding this patient's right to be told, the court also provides guidance on when the post-diagnosis disclosure should occur: 'There are several factors that may affect timing; for example, the anxiety of the patient to be told of the outcome, the patient's condition and ability to participate in the discussion, the seriousness of the information ... and the availability of close family members to offer support and comfort when difficult news has to be given'.

The practical implications of creating this 'right to be told' could take some time to crystallise, and during that interval, an appeal or subsequent judgement overturning this decision may emerge. For instance, is there to be a countervailing right 'not to know'? Does the 'right to be told' create an 'obligation to tell'? And at what threshold of diagnosis does that obligation become engaged; must a serum sodium of 134 mmols/l be disclosed, technically diagnosing 'hyponatraemia'? Any clinician can easily identify simple instances where the right to know, if it exists at all, would in good faith be frustrated by the exigencies of clinical practice.

But be slow to ridicule. Irrespective of the quality of the legal foundations upon which this judgement is based, it should give us pause for thought in terms of how we ensure that our patients are properly informed of clinical findings, and what should be done as a consequence. Irrespective of whether there is a tangible 'right' in these circumstances, it is self-evidently good practice to inform patients of their condition and put into place a strategy for management, of which we are certain they are aware. Few of us would wish to remain oblivious to a malignant diagnosis, perhaps even fewer relishing the risk of no follow-up in those circumstances.

CHAPTER 34

'But All Life Is an Experiment'

B v D [2017] EWCOP 15

D was a 22-year-old Lance Corporal in the British Army, serving three tours in Afghanistan before he was assaulted by a member of his regiment in a bar. He suffered a diffuse axonal injury to his brain, with haematomas surrounding and between and inside the cerebral lobes. During the next year, he was intubated, ventilated, had a tracheostomy and fed via nasogastric tube. Slowly, these supportive measures became unnecessary, and he moved to military rehabilitation. In the following 3 years, his extensive therapies for physical mobility, cognitive/neuropsychological input and speech and language rehabilitation resulted in substantial improvement, but he continues to have significant disabilities and global cognitive impairments. He has reduced attention, concentration, information-processing capacity, memory, executive function and receptive/expressive language.

His mother had identified stem cell therapy as a possible option for treatment of his brain injury. D had expressed a strong desire to receive this, but lacked the capacity to pursue it alone. He had already received financial compensation for his injury, but both the Ministry of Defence (MoD) and the Official Solicitor (acting on his behalf as an incapacitated adult) opposed allowing his funds to be used in this way. These two authorities presented the proposed treatment in Belgrade as 'unproven and risky'; the MoD viewed D's mother's position as her '… strong and natural desire to see her son's condition improve (which has) clouded her ability objectively to judge the likely efficacy of the treatment and the risks to D of undergoing experimental treatment of this kind'. On the contrary, the MoD submitted that the stem cell treatment had no proven medical benefit and was not a viable option. The judge discussed the possible treatment with D on the telephone, and concluded that the wishes he was expressing to receive the treatment were genuinely his own. While D was over-optimistic as to the extent to which the treatment might provide improvement, the judge found that his statements reflected a powerful expression of the strength of his wishes to have treatment. The court found that 'it was almost certain' that D would be much more miserable if he was denied the therapy, and did not accept the proposition that his reaction to refusal would be mere disappointment, but that his adverse reaction would significantly impede and delay his rehabilitation. Equally, the court found that it was undeniable that in the event of side effects or treatment failure, D would also suffer, as could his rehabilitation. But the judge also pointed out that '... for people with disabilities, the removal of such freedom of action as they have to control their own lives may be experienced as an even greater affront than it would be by others who are more fortunate'.

Having balanced the risks and disadvantages of D's options, the court reached a clear conclusion that provisional consent should be given to D to travel to Belgrade for treatment. But this is not before providing stringent conditions to ensure that the clinic fully considered D's details, provided a formal undertaking that he was suitable for stem cell therapy, and would provide detailed plans of both travel and treatment and follow-up arrangements. Finally, the Official Solicitor was authorised to maintain a degree of control over these arrangements.

Underlying this decision were words from an American court a century ago; 'All life is an experiment' as a preface to a more modern decision by a senior English judge:

> Physical health and safety can sometimes be bought at too high a price in happiness and emotional welfare. The emphasis must be on sensible risk appraisal, not striving to avoid all risk, whatever the price, but instead seeking a proper balance and being willing to tolerate manageable or acceptable risks as the price appropriately to be paid in order to achieve some other good; in particular, to achieve the vital good of the elderly or vulnerable person's *happiness*. What good is it making someone safer if it merely makes them miserable?

A good principle on which to base clinical decisions.

CHAPTER 35

Avoid Discouraging Patients from Waiting to Be Treated

Darnley v Croydon Health Services NHST [2018] UKSC 50

In May 2010, Michael Darnley was assaulted; hit on the head. Later, he felt unwell and was taken to hospital by a friend. The patient told the receptionist at the Emergency Department (ED) at 20:26 that he had been attacked and had a very bad headache; 'My head felt really painful and felt like it was in a vice. I just wanted to go home and lie down'. The receptionist told Mr Darnley and his friend that they would have to wait up to 4 or 5 hours to be seen. No more than 19 minutes later, Mr Darnley left the department, and went home, only to call an ambulance at 21:42. A subsequent head computed tomography (CT) scan showed an extra-dural haematoma. Although this was evacuated some 4 hours later, he has permanent brain damage, with a severe dense left hemiplegia.

During litigation, the trial judge found as a fact that had the patient been told from the outset that he would have been seen by a triage nurse within 30 minutes, he would have stayed in the ED, and would have been seen and would have been told to wait for treatment. Following from this, he would have undergone surgery earlier and would have made a 'very nearly full recovery'.

The court was told that while national guidance prescribed clinical triage for head injuries within 15 minutes of arrival at ED, review within 30 minutes was a realistic and reasonable expectation.

The trial judge and subsequent Court of Appeal dismissed the claim on the basis that it was not just, fair and reasonable to impose liability on a hospital for the failure by receptionists to inform the patient of the likely 30-minute waiting time to be seen by a triage nurse. While as a matter of courtesy and 'out of a general spirit of trying to be helpful to the public', information relating to waiting times is provided by hospitals. This provision was not found by the court to be subject to a duty of care in law.

But the Supreme Court disagreed. The court found that telling Mr Darnley he would have to wait 4 or 5 hours to see a doctor was incomplete and misleading, omitting as it did the role of the triage nurse in providing a review within 30 minutes. The court noted the critical finding that it was reasonably foreseeable that a person who believes that they may wait for 4 or 5 hours may decide to leave. In light of this, the provision of misleading information by a receptionist as to time within which clinical assistance might be available equated to substandard care.

But the overarching principle remains that the patient should not be misled – the '4–5 hours' was described in court as 'completely wrong', and from the perspective of any outside observer seems preposterous, an egregious misrepresentation of the service provided by the hospital that he attended.

Plainly, misinformation will have its most potent effect in the context of patients presenting with a rapidly deteriorating clinical situation. Any clinical service with a 'walk-in' element may potentially encounter patients whose untreated condition may cause them harm if they are inadvertently deterred from seeing clinicians. It would be ironic and regrettable if we were to provide less information in a quest to minimise the risk of uttering any misleading words.

The courts recognise the 'colossal' pressures sometimes experienced in emergency and other departments, and that targets may not always be met.

In this instance, the receptionist should have therefore encouraged Mr Darnley to wait to be seen while informing him of the usual plan for review by a triage nurse within 30 minutes. If there had been then some unforeseen delay following his waiting 30 minutes, and he had threatened to leave, she should have repeated the encouragement, and taken reasonable steps to give him a revised time. Discouragement must be avoided.

CHAPTER 36

Mixed Messages

Re SJ [2018] EWCOP 28

In August 2018, a judge decided that a colostomy should be performed on an incapacitated man; in doing so the judge overruled the patient's wishes to avoid the procedure. How can this be justified?

The patient, Mr SJ, was 43 years old, diabetic, incontinent of urine and stool and detained under the Mental Health Act 1983 due to psychosis. He had been admitted to an acute hospital in November 2017 due to sepsis, secondary to a sacral pressure ulcer exposing the bone. During the intervening period, remaining in hospital, SJ's ulcer had partly responded to treatment but at the time of the hearing remained $10 \times 8 \times 3$ cm, exposing the sacrum. He was unable to sense or control defecation due to the neurological complications of his diabetes. As a result, SJ soiled his ulcer every time he opened his bowels, and the court was told that this contamination caused infection and that the ulcer could not heal in the presence of infection. As a consequence, the medical evidence asserted that his life expectancy was 6 months without diversion of the faecal stream, mainly due to the risk of recurrent septicaemia. Alternative methods of reducing soiling were discussed in court, such as rectosigmoid irrigation or thickening stool consistency; it transpired that both methods had been extensively used but that the infection of the ulcer persisted despite them.

The Official Solicitor represented SJ in court. It was accepted that the patient lacked capacity because he was unable to understand or believe information given to him, and unable to weigh the advantages against the disadvantages of colostomy formation. The court was told that SJ did not want the operation because he believed it would cause him further pain. But the doctors told the court that pain was much more likely without the colostomy and both the hospital and the Official Solicitor agreed that the evidence pointed to a 'potential catastrophe' if the colostomy was not performed.

The court scrutinised the meaning of 'best interests', noting that its focus should be directed at how SJ's interests were best served, rather than those of the objective 'reasonable patient' used in other legal circumstances (such as when identifying disclosure for the purposes of consent). In doing so, SJ's wishes and feelings needed to be considered since they were important factors, although not determinative. The strength and consistency of his views and the extent to which these wishes and feelings were or were not rational had to be taken into account, in the context of the clinical circumstances, and crucially, '... the extent to which SJ's wishes and feelings, if given effect to, can be properly accommodated within the court's overall assessment of what is in his best interests'.

When viewed through this prism, the court found that SJ's fears of postoperative pain were unfounded, and that he would both tolerate the colostomy, and be much happier as a result of it. Furthermore, following colostomy, the ulcer would heal, opening the possibility of stoma reversal in the future. The court found colostomy to be lawful.

This is an instance where a patient's wishes were at odds with what manifestly accorded with his welfare. It was straightforward to identify SJ's mistaken belief that postoperative pain would be worse than the suffering entailed by inaction. Having negated this fear, there were no further beliefs or wishes that contradicted the finding that colostomy was in SJ's best interests.

A much more difficult decision would have loomed if the patient's coherent wishes and accurate beliefs betrayed, in reality, his capacity. To watch a patient with capacity die for the want of a colostomy in these circumstances would have been harrowing and profoundly miserable for all involved.

CHAPTER **37**

It Is for Clinicians to Identify Foreseeable Risks

Gail Duce v Worcestershire Acute Hospitals NHST [2018] EWCA Civ 1307

In a recent case, the Court of Appeal distinguished clearly the *clinician's* role in identifying the risks and complications inherent in an intervention from the *patient's* role in deciding which risks she is willing to run. The distinction is important since the patient's choice may be influenced by considerations that are not 'medical'.

Mrs Duce, 41 years old, had presented in 2008 with gynaecological symptoms including lower back pain. She sought a total abdominal hysterectomy to resolve these. Her family doctor had noted her insistence, notwithstanding that this involved major surgery with associated risks. She wanted it 'all taken away'. Gynaecologists initially recommended less invasive management of her symptoms, but in a review clinic 3 weeks later the patient again confirmed that she would not consider preliminary alternative treatments, only then to find they had failed. In preparation for surgery, the risks and complications of total abdominal hysterectomy and bilateral salpingo-oophorectomy were disclosed, including the risk that the operation might not relieve the pains with which she presented. But the surgical registrar who dealt with the consent accepted that she would not in 2008 have disclosed that there was a risk of developing chronic and/or neuropathic pain as a result of the surgery. She would merely have warned of transient postoperative pain.

Following surgery, Mrs Duce suffered abdominal wall pain that was 'significantly different' from her preoperative symptoms. Experts in pain management agreed that her subsequent course was consistent with chronic postsurgical pain. Mrs Duce claimed that if she had been warned of the risk of nerve damage and chronic postsurgical pain, she would not have proceeded with the surgery.

The court heard that the Royal College of Obstetricians and Gynaecologists Guidance in 2009 (which it was agreed would reflect best practice in 2008) recommended the disclosure of the likelihood of '… numbness, tingling or burning sensation around the scar … that could take weeks or months to resolve'. But the judge noted that neither chronic nor neuropathic pain was referred to in the Guidance, and that the claimant and defending expert witnesses in gynaecology agreed that chronic postsurgical pain was not common knowledge among gynaecologists in 2008.

Accordingly, the court found that since the reasonable gynaecologist in 2008 would not have been aware of chronic postsurgical pain founded on nerve injury during total abdominal hysterectomy, there could not have been a duty to disclose that risk during the process of obtaining consent.

For these reasons, among others, Mrs Duce's claim was dismissed.

The case serves as a powerful reminder that the clinician must set out risks to which a reasonable person in the patient's position would have attached significance, or risks to which the doctor was or should have been aware that the patient would be likely to attach significance. By contrast, it is only the patient who can then choose whether to run these risks. This choice is not one that a clinician can anticipate for the patient, since only the patient can bring into this consideration all other aspects of their life that may have a bearing on this decision.

But in the same breath, it was equally acknowledged by the courts that the *task of identifying those risks* which foreseeably result from an intervention is one for the clinician, in this case the gynaecologist. If, as in this case, the complication that crystallised was not at the time of disclosure for consent a recognised association of hysterectomy that the reasonable gynaecologist should have been aware of, it would have been unjust to expect the doctor to have mentioned it.

CHAPTER 38

Separating Twins

Re A (Minors) (Conjoined Twins: Surgical Separation) [2001] Fam 147

Nearly 20 years ago, a court was faced with an agonising decision – whether the proposed separation of conjoined twins was lawful. A court decision was necessary; the parents opposed the separation because the operation would lead to the immediate death of one of their twins. This dilemma could re-emerge at any moment, so the decision merits study.

The case, *Re A*, concerned Jodie and Mary, born to devout Catholic parents. The girls each had their own brain, heart, lungs and vital organs; and each had four limbs. But the court was told that Mary's cardiorespiratory system was insufficient to support life; she remained alive only because of their connected circulations. Jodie's aorta supplied that of her sister; and their inferior cavae were distally united into a common channel. If Mary had been born as an independent baby, she would not have lived after cessation of placental circulation.

Without separation, the surgeons predicted that Mary would die within 3–6 months, followed within hours by her sister, who would exsanguinate into her dead sister's circulation. Surgical separation in the neonatal period was feasible, and Jodie would be able to live a relatively normal life, but Mary would die within minutes of the division of the aortic connection. Their parents opposed the operation, believing their children's fate should be left to God and that terminating Mary's life was wrong.

The legal 'formula' for murder in England requires an intention to kill (as well as an act that causes death) to be established. The court in *Re A* recognised that each twin was a separate person for the purposes of homicide and that both girls had to be accorded equal rights to life, but considered Mary's death to be justified as 'the lesser of two evils', declaring separation lawful. Nonetheless, the court conceded that the surgeons would by performing the operation 'intend to kill' Mary since her death would be virtually certain once her aorta was clamped. Although one of the reasons for the court's decision was that the surgeons could rely on a defence of necessity (to save Jodie's life), subsequent legal argument suggests that this defence may no longer be available.

Courts have held that the greater the scope for genuine doubt as to where a child's best interests lie, the greater the expectation that the difficult decision will be taken by her parents.

Academic lawyers have suggested that seeking to justify giving priority to the welfare of one or the other twin was an exercise too finely balanced for clinicians or judges to arrive at a conclusion with certainty. Put bluntly, it remains uncertain that either twin could mount a strong case that she should thrive at the expense of her sister. In these circumstances, the justification to usurp the parents' settled decision to refuse surgery evaporates. At the same time, sociological evidence hints at conjoined twins' profound disinclination to be separated. Plainly, this evidence requires close scrutiny.

Taken together, considerable doubt is cast upon the proposition that the judgement in *Re A* can be relied upon by contemporary surgeons faced with the prospect of needing to sacrifice the life of one twin for the benefit of another. It is arguable that if this sacrifice was made in 2019, the surgeons would need to convince a jury either that the elements of murder were not made out or, alternatively, that a defence against that charge was both available and applicable.

By extension, if the idea that enduring conjoinity was valued by and valuable to conjoined twins withstood critical analysis, courts might view any separation, whether or not imminent death of one twin was anticipated, with sufficient anxiety to defer a decision to separate until the children had capacity to make the choice for themselves.

CHAPTER 39

Body Modification

R v BM [2018] EWCA Crim 560

All those in clinical professions seek consent for what would otherwise be an unlawful touch. As citizens contemplate body modification, are there interventions which cannot be made lawful by consent?

In 1604, one man persuaded another to slice off his left hand, optimising sympathy while begging; 200 years later, a dentist extracted the front teeth of a musketeer, preventing him from biting open the paper cartridge containing gunpowder and ball, rendering him incapable of loading his rifle, unfit for combat duty. In neither case did consent save the 'clinician' from conviction.

Both of these injuries equated to serious injury from which flows the risk of unanticipated further disease and possibly death. This imposes a substantial cost on society as a whole. For this reason, Parliament regulates (albeit loosely) piercing and tattooing in adults, while proscribing tattooing in children.

More recently, the courts have held that causing serious injury outside medical practice is unlawful, irrespective of consent, finding that the infliction of facial scars on a child's cheek is a crime. This illustrates that if the law condemns an act, consent does not provide an answer to the criminal charge.

To what extent do the courts consider body modification lawful?

In a criminal appeal case, a registered tattooist and piercer included 'body modification' in his public offering. He found himself charged with three charges of wounding with intent to inflict grievous bodily harm since he had removed an ear and a nipple, and split a third customer's tongue into the forked reptilian style. It was accepted that in each case consent had been provided; the question for the court was whether that consent made these excisions or incisions lawful. The Crown Court judge who first heard the case held that consent provided no defence to these serious injuries.

The left ear was removed from a Mr Lott without anaesthetic. Both defence and prosecution accepted that this posed the risk of both hearing loss and injury to the facial nerve. The upshot included difficulty in wearing spectacles or hearing aids. The nipple/areola complex was excised, leaving a linear scar and resulting in asymmetry.

The tongue splitting was performed using a scalpel without anaesthetic; aside from the foreseeable risks to airway and circulation during the procedure, speech and feeding would be affected.

The court noted that if any of these customers had performed the procedure upon themselves, no crime would have been committed. Nonetheless, the judges could find no reason why body modification should be equated to surgery. For the non-surgeon, consent provides no defence to the person who inflicts violence causing actual bodily harm or a more serious injury. The body modifier's conviction was upheld.

Many surgical acts would be crimes if done by anyone other than a surgeon. Since this case provides further evidence that consent is not sufficient to make serious injury lawful, it also confirms that proper medical treatment, with consent as a prerequisite, is in a category of its own. One reason (of many) for this distinction is that a doctor will be equipped to consider whether their patient has capacity for the treatment they seek.

Procedures performed by surgeons for body dysmorphic disorder may not have been tested in court. But it can be seen that a serious injury such as limb amputation would need to be balanced by its prevention of an equally serious harm to justify inclusion in the category where with consent, the procedure is deemed reasonable medical treatment. Where the patient with capacity in desperation wishes to be rid of a leg that is distressing him, it may not be for the criminal law to go behind the patient's autonomous judgement of how best to make him healthy.

This remains an area of practice fraught with anxiety for clinicians facing unusual requests for modification. How, for instance, should the clinician deal with the Paralympian seeking surgical modification to further optimise his competitive potential? A criminal case identifying 'serious injury' as something against which consent is no defence provides guidance as to circumstances where a clinician should seek early advice.

CHAPTER 40

Seeking the Approval of a Court for Paternity Testing

DCC v NLH [2019] EWCOP 9

In a judgement handed down in 2019, the Court of Protection made an order concerning a man in the late stages of a degenerative neurological disease. The patient, NLH, had at an earlier stage of his illness made it clear to a social worker and a manager at his nursing home that he wanted his child to be made aware of this disease and that since the child may have inherited the illness, he should have the opportunity in due course to decide for himself whether to be tested.

At that stage, no action was taken to inform NLH's child. Later, a Family Court declared that the outcome of DNA tests on NLH would be of the utmost importance for any of his children. This would not only allow disputes over paternity to be settled, but also (should NLH's paternity be confirmed), any child of his could at some stage be made aware of his or her father's heritable disease, for the reasons that NLH had expressed while he retained his capacity.

As the legal process to obtain his DNA proceeded, NLH deteriorated rapidly, now lacking capacity to consent for the buccal swabs to be taken from him. As a matter of urgency, lest he die before these could be taken, it was decided to make an application to the out-of-hours judge in the Court of Protection. The application to take the sample and test the DNA was supported by the Official Solicitor, who acted on NLH's behalf. All agreed that there were overwhelmingly strong arguments to establish whether he was the father of the child.

The court made a declaration that these activities were lawful. It is understandable that the Local Authority dealing with the family made such an application since the request for paternity testing would need to be dealt with in a higher court. But absent the need for the Family Court to deal with paternity for other reasons, the 'overwhelmingly strong arguments' for testing NLH would, if he had been in a hospital setting, have made it very likely that the test would have been performed without an application to any court. Such a decision would have taken his wishes and feelings into consideration. His family agreed that testing was in NLH's interests and those of his children, and there would be clinical consensus.

After these proceedings had commenced, but before the court order was made, an employee of the DNA testing company took the sample from NLH with the agreement of his family, but with neither his consent (lacking capacity to provide consent) nor the approval of the court.

As an important aside, the judge took a very dim view of this behaviour. Despite an application to the court and the case's listing for hearing in the Court of Protection, the buccal smear was taken from NLH before the order was made. The judge made it crystal clear that in these circumstances such practice was unlawful: '... there is always a judge of the Family Division on duty ... twenty-four hours a day, every day of the year, to deal with urgent applications, usually by telephone'. This is a serious matter, potentially incurring financial compensation if a breach of the patient's human rights is established.

We all need to remember this: if we choose to make an application to court to determine whether our clinical plans are lawful, we then must sit on our hands until the order we seek is made.

We much more often ponder patients' advance refusals, such as refusing blood transfusion, rather than advance requests for treatment. A request made in advance of becoming incapacitated should be taken into account in any best interests decision; an example of this is a request for delivery by caesarean section. Refusals are articulated through Advance Decisions on paper, or in person, through the appointment of a Lasting Power of Attorney. By contrast, NLH's assertions to the care manager and social worker, although falling short of consent to a buccal swab, nevertheless give a firm indication that he wanted his children to be made aware of their risk of inherited disease. This was a powerful oral statement of his wishes and feelings.

The Mental Capacity Act 2005 places special emphasis on any written statements that a patient makes before losing capacity since they provide an opportunity to understand the patient's wishes. Written statements of this type should be taken as seriously as those made by patients with capacity.

CHAPTER 41

Children Refusing Treatment

Re P (A Minor) [1986] 1 FLR 272
Re W (A Minor) (Medical Treatment: Court's Jurisdiction)
[1993] Fam 64 CA
Re M (Medical Treatment: Consent) [1999] 2 FLR 1097

'Competent Minors' (*Gillick*[*] competent children under 16 and young people 16 and 17 years of age, the latter who are presumed to have capacity) successfully refuse treatment in the National Health Service countless times every day. They decline oral medications, ignore the advice of physiotherapists and refuse point-blank to be anaesthetised for operations that could improve the quality of their lives. In each circumstance, the clinicians and parents come to a decision as to how to deal with the refusal on the basis of pragmatism. There is often an alternative to treatment which may be acceptable: a different oral form of drug, a reduced frequency of treatments, or simply resignation on behalf of those caring for the person that since it is rarely feasible to force her to acquiesce, any compliance is better than none. In surgical terms, we often wait until the symptoms from the yet-to-be-operated hernia or ingrowing toenail or recurrently infected cyst get to the point of persuading the child or young person that the proffered treatment is less bad than the disease. In reality, the vast majority of refusals by competent and capacitous minors are dealt with in this way. The underlying truth is that adults are powerless in modern society to insist on compliance in these circumstances, and that the long-term consequence of temporarily obtaining compliance by force will be to disenfranchise the eventual adult from clinical care, perhaps resulting in serious enduring harm.

But having reflected that pragmatic reality, where do clinicians stand when the competent minor refuses life-saving treatment? Perhaps unsurprisingly, the short answer is that the refusal of a competent minor, and if need be that of her parents, can be overridden by a court if it is in her best interests to do so. It follows that the right of child and parent to refuse treatment is not absolute. The court is bound to have regard to the ascertainable wishes and feelings of the competent child or capacitious young person and will not

---
[*] Gillick v West Norfolk & Wisbech AHA [1986] AC 112

lightly override their refusal if the minor's decision is sensible or the treatment invasive. In the case of a 16-year-old orphaned girl called W, who had been unsuccessfully fostered and then suffered further misfortunes, a local authority was seeking the court's agreement to admit her to a unit where she could be compulsorily fed. Her anorexia was threatening her life. W said that as she was 16 years old, with a statutory right to consent to treatment, she also had the right to refuse it. While the High Court found that she did have sufficient understanding to make an informed decision, it nevertheless held that this could be overridden, so her case was appealed.

In finding that W's refusal could be overridden, the Court of Appeal revealed its approach to balancing the under-18's autonomy against the risks involved in its observance: 'Good parenting involves giving minors as much rope as they can handle without an unacceptable risk that they will hang themselves'. Put another way, 'The first and paramount consideration (of the court) is the well-being, welfare or interests (of the minor) and I regard it as self-evident that this involves giving them the maximum degree of decision-making which is prudent. Prudence does not involve avoiding all risk, but it does involve avoiding risks which, if they eventuate, may have irreparable consequence or which are disproportionate to the benefits which would accrue from taking them'.

In practice, the court is unlikely to overrule a competent minor's decision in the ordinary run of surgical/dental/medical treatment, despite its power to do so. Furthermore, courts have supported competent children who were in conflict with their parents, adopting and upholding the children's views on serious treatment. In the case of P, a 15-year-old competent girl of 'strong personality and mature views', the child's wish to have an abortion was opposed by her Seventh-Day Adventist parents; the court nonetheless directed that the abortion was lawful.

But when the risk of a competent minor's death turns on his or her refusal of treatment, it is generally the duty of the court to preserve life and ensure as far as possible that the child reaches adulthood. For this reason, despite the ubiquitous pragmatic acceptance by clinicians of refusals of routine treatment by this group of patients, competent minors have invariably had their refusals of compulsory feeding and blood transfusions overridden by English courts.

The judiciary's view on refusal of solid organ transplant remains to be seen. Although 20 years ago, a 15 year old's preliminary refusal of heart transplant was overridden in a case known as *Re M*, it appears that she later acquiesced. Jurists are acutely aware of the gravity and practicality of enforcing not simply the transplant, but the management of the implicit subsequent lifelong immunosuppression. Just how will this be achieved, given the dissenter's trenchant opposition? And then there are the consequences of starkly practical refusal: Rejection of the precious grafted organ equates as a loss to a different person who would have willingly received it. The court must be reluctant to impose their powers in this most distant orbit of tolerable paternalism.

These cases demonstrate that while courts take steps to ascertain and consider the views of the competent child, the eventual outcome reflects that the child's view is not considered determinative. Perhaps in transplant cases an exception might be made.

CHAPTER 42

Can We Rely on Our Advance Decisions?

NHS Cumbria CCG v Mrs Jillian Rushton & Ors [2018] EWCOP 41

Advance Decisions allow an adult to refuse life-saving treatment in a future where they envisage they may lack capacity to deliver that refusal personally. Although an advance decision allows us to refuse any treatment, it is the rejection of life-prolonging treatment that commands the attention of all clinicians, rightly so.

In a case heard in the Court of Protection just before Christmas 2018, it became clear that Mrs Jillian Rushton, a retired nurse, had in 2014 signed an advance decision. These are her words:

> … On collapse, I do not wish to be resuscitated by any means … I am refusing all treatment. Even if my life is at risk. … In all circumstances of collapse that put my life at risk, this direction is to be applied.

These words are of great importance since they provide explicit instructions from a person with capacity who intends to influence her future treatment. One of the conditions that must be met by those drawing up an advance decision is that 'specified medical treatments' that the person wishes to refuse must be identified. Mrs Rushton's advance decision was sent to her general practitioner (GP) and filed. It should be noted that she did not specify a particular medical treatment, such as intubation, ventilation, renal replacement or gastrostomy tube placement; instead she refused 'all treatment'.

Her health and cognitive function then progressively declined, culminating 18 months later in a fall and major head injury. The severity of her injury initially prompted palliative care, but she improved and within a few days nasogastric feeding was started.

The court found no evidence that the hospital was made aware of the advance decision, either by the general practice or the family members.

As her condition improved, the decision was taken to replace her nasogastric tube with a gastrostomy, in part to allow her to be looked after at home by her son. It seems that the change to a percutaneous endoscopic gastrostomy tube occurred almost simultaneously with a call initially from hospital to the GP, thence the GP to the hospital, probably in relation to the possible existence of an advance decision. The hospital's record of the latter call shows that the GP relayed, '... the only ADR (Advance Decision) in place is in regard to *do not resuscitate*'.

The court found that at some point in the relaying of its content, Mrs R's advance decision had been misinterpreted, and that she would have intended to avoid gastrostomy placement. The judge went further, noting the 'onerous' burden on the GP to ensure that (once lodged in the practice records) wherever possible, the advance decision document should be made available and placed within the hospital records. The court noted that '... It need hardly be said that it will rarely, if ever, be sufficient to summarise an advance decision in a telephone conversation'.

This judicial instruction may be difficult to implement. Parliament brought the Mental Capacity Act 2005 into existence together with a Code of Practice, but created no machinery or suggestions as to how the advance decision might be delivered to the hands of the clinicians responsible for treating the patients. This is in contrast to the register of Lasting Powers of Attorney. In a technological age, a paper document sits uncomfortably within the system; the practicalities of 'flagging up' the existence of almost countless individually significant considerations relating to patient safety and welfare (not least in the field of medications) continue to cause hospitals great concern. Equally, it seems likely that within general practice, maintaining alerts relating to the existence (and continuing applicability) of advance decisions may not be as straightforward as it sounds in a courtroom.

As an aside, if the hospital clinicians had received Mrs Rushton's advance decision, although its presence may have ultimately resulted in the avoidance of a gastrostomy tube, the text of the refusal would have necessitated anxious and cautious analysis. In particular, she was refusing 'all treatment'. Did Mrs Rushton mean also to refuse palliative care, which would otherwise enable her to retain dignity, comfort and consolation at the end of her life? Since that could be the effect of the words in her advance decision.

The *court* found that 'all treatment' included gastrostomy feeding, but defined 'all' no further. Where should a *clinician* draw a line between what Mrs R likely meant to proscribe while maintaining treatments that it is foreseeable, in reality, she would have wanted, such as the benefits of hospice care?

If the existence of this advance decision in Mrs R's circumstances had been recognised, it is likely in any case to have led to an approach to the Court of Protection as to the extent of the treatments to which Mrs Rushton had intended her refusals to apply.

As a more general point, the advance decision has proved a problematic instrument. Patients, lacking clairvoyance, often fail to identify relevant specific treatments that they wish to refuse in the future because they have as yet no idea of the clinical circumstances of their final illness. In the absence of a central electronic register of advance decisions, clinicians are often (perhaps usually) oblivious of their existence. But even if one is identified, questions relating to the patient's true intentions persist.

CHAPTER 43

Is There a Role for 'Next of Kin'?

No case

Whether admission to our hospital is recorded on paper or electronically, we faithfully record the patient's 'next of kin'. Is this useful information?

Patients may naturally wish to identify a person for the hospital to contact, useful for arranging their discharge, or to deal with other domestic arrangements. The clinicians will also wish to have a nominated person with whom they can communicate if their patient deteriorates to the point where his or her capacity is lost. Who should the patient, on being admitted, identify as their next of kin?

The simple answer is anyone they choose, ideally a person who is readily contactable and who the patient is confident will act in a sensible way. The difficulty is that since the 'next of kin' has no legal status, being undefined in English law, there is no other guidance we can give. In particular, there is no distinction between blood relatives, family, friends and acquaintances. The person who will best do the job may be unrelated to the patient – perhaps it is the man who walks her dog.

Since the role is not defined in law, it is unsurprising that the *next of kin* has no powers. However, clinicians must seek information as to the wishes, feelings and beliefs of an incapacitated patient. It is sensible to begin this search with the person nominated as next of kin, although this quest may well become more extensive.

We have all seen the distress and disruption caused when a patient identifies as their next of kin someone of whom factions in the family strongly disapprove. This can lead to unseemly dispute, and clinicians should liaise with the nominee, while advising them to share the information they have been given with the rest of the family. This is doubtless a difficult situation, sharpened by the general public's certain but mistaken belief that the next of kin has determinative status.

A rather easier situation arises where the patient has arrived lacking capacity, unable to pronounce on 'next of kin'. The hospital record may thus stand empty, or the most interested accompanying person (relative or otherwise) may have identified themselves, and now appear on the record. This self-appointment may not sit well with subsequently attending family members. In either situation, all those who befriend the patient should be given the same information, bearing in mind the obvious rules on confidentiality. Since the patient has not identified a particular spokesman, we are unable to do so on his or her behalf. In practical terms, when faced with numerous befrienders, the simplest course is to suggest to the first few seeking information that they spread what news can be disclosed to those interested.

The *next of kin* originated in English property disputes in the sixteenth century, and to this day provides in American statute an order of precedence for those relatives wishing to inherit property from a person who dies intestate. The situation is similar in Ireland. By contrast, English intestacy rules stipulate who will inherit an individual's estate, but not in terms of 'next of kin'. The phrase has not appeared in English statute for many years. The Mental Health Act 1959 (and its successors) defines 'nearest relative', while the Human Tissue Act 2004 notes 'qualifying relationships', to name only two of many statutes where interpersonal relationships are of vital importance, but in which no recognition is given to *next of kin*. Judges use the phrase in court, but only as plain language, giving it no specific legal meaning.

Any adult (including a clinician) might ponder who they would wish to nominate in the event of their own incapacity. One answer lies in the Lasting Power of Attorney (LPA), a creation of the Mental Capacity Act 2005. The LPA allows us all to identify a person who can represent our wishes (and in some circumstances our refusal of treatment) on the advent of our incapacity. This provides the donee of the LPA with powers entirely unavailable to the *next of kin*.

CHAPTER 44

Preaching to Patients

Kuteh v Dartford & Gravesham NHST [2019] EWCA Civ 818

In a recent case from an Employment Tribunal, a band 5 nurse appealed against her dismissal for initiating discussions about religion with patients. Initially, a junior intensive care unit (ICU) sister, the nurse, a committed Christian, had been transferred to work in a surgical pre-assessment role. The pre-assessment included an enquiry about patients' religion, although it provided no invitation for further discussion of the subject. Some months after her reassignment, staff began to receive complaints from patients about the nurse raising matters of religion with them. One complaint related to a patient facing bowel resection for cancer, who was told that his survival would be more likely if he prayed to God. Other complaints were less specific, reflecting patients' irritation or awkwardness at what they saw as unwarranted and unwelcome probing or advice on religious themes; they '... didn't like (her) preaching'.

As a consequence, the nurse was told by her Matron that '... a number of patients were offended that you spent a fair amount of the allocated pre-assessment time on the subject (of religion)'. She gave an assurance that she would not engage patients on this topic unless asked to do so. Nonetheless, the nurse subsequently gave a patient a Bible and offered to pray for her. Another patient complained that the nurse was preaching at her, making her feel uncomfortable. A further patient was offered a Bible, being told that the only way to get to the Lord was through Jesus. On having his hand gripped, he was asked to sing the 23rd Psalm with her; thus astonished, he did so, accompanying her for the first verse. He described this encounter as 'very bizarre'.

The court noted the nurse's plea that her employer failed to recognise her genuine attempts to comfort her patients. But equally, the court found no dispute that any person being pre-assessed for surgery was foreseeably '... worried, possibly suffering from stress, and potentially vulnerable'. The nurse had been given a direct and lawful instruction to desist from initiating religious discussions with her patients, and acknowledged her disobedience.

The Court of Appeal upheld the Employment Tribunal's decision to dismiss the nurse. The court made clear the importance of the right to freedom of religion, and found no blanket ban on religious speech in the workplace imposed by her employer. Citing the Nursing and Midwifery Council (NMC) Code Para 20, in relation to upholding the reputation of the profession, the court noted that nurses and midwives must make sure that they do not express personal beliefs (including political, religious or moral beliefs) to people in an *inappropriate* way. The distinction between inappropriate and appropriate expressions of religious beliefs in a clinical setting is echoed by the General Medical Council.

The case provides a timely reminder to all clinicians as to the importance of limiting the expressions of our political (and religious) views to those that are appropriate. As is so often the case, this judgement identifies the inappropriate but leaves to a clinician the definition of the appropriate. While entirely consistent with the ancient principle that all that is not proscribed by English law remains lawful, this case provides us no help with these purely subjective judgements. Unsurprisingly, the safest approach is caution when initiating sometimes necessary discussions of religion, politics or morality with those for whom we have a clinical responsibility.

CHAPTER 45

Deceiving Patients

University Hospitals Derby & Burton NHSFT v J [2019] EWCOP 16

All clinicians are well aware that patients must not be tricked or cheated into receiving treatment that they would otherwise refuse to undergo. Clinical regulators make this crystal clear. Recent revelations concerning patients who were tricked into having entirely unnecessary intimate examinations, or surgery, underline why deception is detestable and harmful to public confidence in medicine. In this context, it could be construed as a criminal act. Can deception ever be justified?

The case of Anne, a young woman with autism and a severe learning disability, was recently heard in court. She lacked capacity to make decisions about her medical treatment. Anne had a marked aversion to leaving her home, or to travel by road. The court found that she would not do so willingly.

Since her menarche, she had suffered very severe distress at the sight of her own menstrual bleeding. Her distress was expressed as aggressive and challenging behaviour, exacerbated by hormonal fluctuation. Despite an exhaustive range of treatments (most recently 3 monthly Decapeptyl injections) during her teenage and young adult life, this problem culminated in severe episodes of mental illness. As the limitations of these treatments and the risks of their side effects became ever more apparent, the question of hysterectomy came increasingly to the fore. Hysterectomy, removing the possibility of menstruation, would permanently abolish her primary source of distress, and simultaneous oophorectomy would ameliorate her challenging cyclical behaviour. Taken together, all were agreed that this surgery would reduce the chances of recurrence of her mental illness.

The hospital trust looking after Anne thus sought a declaration that removal of her uterus, fallopian tubes and ovaries would be in her best interests. Anticipating that Anne would refuse to travel to hospital, the Trust proposed giving her a sedative, while pretending that her usual injection of Decapeptyl was being administered. The patient's parents supported this proposal, noting that they believed it was overdue, frustrated that it should have been undertaken 5 years previously. The Official Solicitor, acting for Anne, noted that she was unable to express a clear view about the surgery, but that she had indicated that she wanted to avoid menstruation or childbearing.

The judge found that deceiving her into accepting sedation would facilitate transport, anaesthesia and surgery, minimising the impact that this sequence of events would have upon her. In declaring the proposed plan to be in her best interests, he found that 'the means is completely justified by the end'.

Such an approach mirrors previous judgements where incapacitated patients have been deceived into accepting treatments that they would have otherwise refused. Examples include a woman who did not believe she had uterine cancer in whom it was declared lawful to mislead into having extirpative surgery and a man who needed to have excisional biopsy of a breast carcinoma, where it was feared that he would 'go berserk' if he was told the truth about what was about to happen to him.

Deception (given in the dictionary as 'seizing from, cheating or trickery') is plainly closely allied to covert treatment (defined in terms such as hidden, covered and secret). It is well recognised that covert treatment must conform to the principles of the Mental Capacity Act 2005. Perhaps deception is different from covert treatment, since it is foreseeable that the patient eventually will come to realise the trickery, albeit it rooted in benevolent intent, to which they have been subjected. An unanticipated scar or the exchange of a familiar subcutaneous lump for an unwelcome fresh incision may give the game away. Covert treatment, on the other hand, where it has been found lawful, in a person's best interests, to hide antipsychotic sedation in a strongly flavoured drink, is less likely to later become obvious to the patient. Since deception may thus be inherently more objectionable to a patient (should they ever come to realise that they were duped) than covert treatment, it is vital that clinicians should seek independent assurance, almost certainly from the Court of Protection, before adopting such measures.

CHAPTER 46

Determining Incapacity

Heart of England NHSFT v JB [2014] EWHC 324 COP

In 2014, a judge's decision provided us with helpful guidance as to how to diagnose incapacity. The case related to JB, a 62-year-old woman with paranoid schizophrenia; it was agreed that she lacked insight, and thus capacity to make decisions about treatment for her mental illness. JB also had a gangrenous foot; she was a hypertensive, insulin-dependent diabetic who smoked heavily. The foot had become ulcerated in May 2013; by August 2013 gangrene had set in, and the court was told that auto-amputation was considered her best option. During the subsequent autumn, the foot, not yet separated, was the source of an ascending infection. Surgical amputation to protect the remaining leg was mooted, but JB did not agree. There was no clinical consensus over her capacity; some thought she was simply making an unwise decision, whilst others considered she lacked capacity. The latter view was based on the observation that while JB could understand and retain information related to proposed alternative treatments, her long-standing pattern of minimising and underplaying concerns relating to her health compromised her ability to weigh opposing risks and benefits. This, some argued, rendered her unable to reach a decision.

The decision to amputate was deferred, but when the foot eventually separated in January 2014 it left an open wound, and distal leg amputation was again recommended, although the court found no settled plan as to the proposed level of resection. During the ensuing discussions relating to JB's capacity, the need for 'certainty of her capacity ... or certainty she lacks capacity' was recorded in the hospital notes. By February, the hospital applied for a declaration that JB lacked capacity to make a decision about serious medical treatment, and that a through-knee amputation, together with any necessary sedation, was in her best interests.

The court set out several principles: Firstly, that '... the temptation to base a judgement of a person's capacity upon whether they seem to have made a good or bad decision, and in particular upon whether they have accepted or rejected medical advice, is absolutely to be avoided. That would be to put the cart before the horse or, expressed another way, to allow the tail of welfare to wag the dog of capacity. Any tendency in this direction risks infringing the rights of that group of persons who, though vulnerable, are capable of making their own decisions. Many who suffer from mental illness are well able to make decisions about their medical treatment, and it is important not to make unjustified assumptions to the contrary'.

Secondly, what was required of JB was a broad general understanding of the kind that is expected from the population at large. Clinicians must also remember that common strategies employed by all citizens to deal with unpalatable dilemmas, such as indecision, avoidance and vacillation are not to be confused with incapacity ... we should not ask more of people whose capacity is questioned than of those whose capacity is beyond doubt. Thirdly, the judge cautioned us to remember that the presumption a patient has capacity is displaced *on the balance of probabilities*; we are not searching for *certainty*, or for a demonstration that a patient can *fully* understand, retain and weigh. Such formulations do not sit well with the requirements of the Mental Capacity Act 2005. Finally, as a more general point, the court warned us of the danger that the patient '... is regarded as capable of making a decision that follows medical advice but incapable of making one that does not'.

Applying these principles to the evidence, the court found that it did not follow that JB's lack of insight into her mental illness correlated with incapacity to decide over amputation and that it had not ever been established that she lacked capacity to consent or refuse surgery. On the contrary, the evidence established her capacity to choose whether or not to have surgery, and she was free to make that choice. It appeared, by the end of the hearing, that she was discussing the possibility of a below-knee operation with her doctors. She was therefore preparing to consent, rather than having amputation forced upon her.

CHAPTER 47

Reasons for Refusing Blood?

Manchester University NHSFT v DE [2019] EWHC 1317 Fam

A middle-aged woman fell down the stairs of a bus. She suffered fractures of her femur and tibia and was awaiting open fixation of these bones. Her surgeon predicted a 50% chance of the patient (D) requiring blood product transfusion.

It transpired that D and her mother were both Jehovah's Witnesses. The mother was a committed Witness, and she did not believe that it was in her daughter's best interests to have a blood transfusion, since this was contrary to the belief of their religious group. D had autism and mild learning difficulties, and the hospital asserted that she lacked capacity to decide whether or not to have a transfusion.

It was for this reason, that the hospital applied to the Court of Protection to seek a declaration that it would be lawful to transfuse if need be. The court heard that two clinicians had assessed D's capacity, and agreed that she did not appear to understand that she might need a transfusion, nor could she link the need for an operation with the potential for also needing blood products transfused. The patient was nevertheless aware that her leg was broken, that she needed surgery and that without surgery she could not go home. D was clear that she wanted surgery and she wanted to go home; she expressly said that she did not want to die. The court found that she could not retain, use or weigh the information relating to the consequences of refusing blood, thus lacking capacity for this decision.

The court reviewed the evidence on D's beliefs and her commitment to the Jehovah's Witnesses. D attended religious services. She could recite the scriptures but gave no indication of whether she understood them or believed them, or the extent to which they played an important role in her life. D could not explain why blood transfusion was prohibited under her religion. The court found that 'although D described herself as a Jehovah's Witness she was not someone for whom those beliefs were central to her personality or sense of identity'. This view was supported by those of the Official Solicitor, noting that she did not strongly identify herself with the beliefs of the Jehovah's Witnesses.

Having concluded that D's *religious* beliefs were not being overridden, the court then turned its attention to the issue of whether there was disproportionate interference with D's rights to *cultural* beliefs, lest her opposition to blood transfusion be viewed as cultural rather than religious. It became clear that she was 'not too concerned about having a transfusion'. D's mother would not consent to a transfusion but neither did she object to it if necessary. She supported D having the operation.

The court did not get a sense that D would '... feel deeply upset ... or that she would feel a deep conflict' with her religious beliefs if surgery and transfusion were declared lawful. Accordingly, the judge had 'no hesitation' in finding that the operation was in D's best interests.

The judgement in no way rides roughshod over the respect clinicians must give to the refusal of blood by any adult with capacity. But it does focus attention on the extent to which, when dealing with a patient brought up within a Jehovah's Witness household, an incapacitated patient understands the implications of refusing blood products.

Nor does the decision alter our approach to any patient who lacks capacity to refuse blood, despite the existence of an order allowing us to administer it. Naturally, we should take every opportunity to refrain from the administration of blood products while that avoidance remains consistent with the patient's best interests.

CHAPTER 48

Justifying the Termination of a Pregnancy

Re AB (Termination of Pregnancy) [2019] EWCA Civ 1215

AB is 24 years old. Born in Nigeria, she was adopted at birth by CD, though lived in Nigeria for many years while her adoptive mother worked in London as a midwife. When she was 12 years old, AB moved to London, and it became apparent that she had a significant developmental delay, an IQ in the range of 35–49. In association with this she has profound behavioural difficulties, her mood managed by medication. Established in London, she lived largely with her grandmother, although CD lived with them for substantial periods.

In May 2017, her grandmother died, causing AB great loss and distress. Henceforth, she has lived with her mother. During prolonged leave in Nigeria, AB fell pregnant, diagnosed by her mother at around 11 weeks' gestation in the middle of April 2019. It was inevitably concluded that AB lacked capacity to decide whether to continue with the pregnancy; the Trust mooted the idea of termination. CD was wholly opposed to termination on both religious and cultural grounds. A Roman Catholic, she observed that in Nigeria terminating a pregnancy is '… simply unheard of'. Four weeks later CD took her daughter to the hospital with all her possessions packed in three suitcases and two rucksacks, telling the hospital she was 'handing over care' of her daughter. She felt she could not support AB in having a termination. Subsequently, AB has lived in residential care.

The Trust made an application to the High Court at 18 weeks' gestation, seeking a declaration that in the circumstances termination was lawful, consistent with the Abortion Act 1967. The Trust concluded that termination was in AB's best interests. The hearing commenced when AB was in her 23rd week.

The Official Solicitor represented AB, and supported her mother in opposing an order that would result in termination. While the local authority was neutral, AB's social worker also opposed termination. The judge recorded CD's view that her daughter would be very upset by having a termination, but never did she thereafter weigh this in the balance when considering AB's best interests. Equally, the judge gave no weight to the evidence of the social worker who had known AB for 2 years, and who had told the court that it would be in her best interests to have the baby. This contrasted with medical evidence that after full-term delivery, AB might suffer psychosis, although acknowledged that quantification of such an illness was unknowable.

The court was told that AB's termination of pregnancy would be a two-stage surgical procedure over 2 days, performed under general anaesthetic. AB would be told that they were 'taking the baby away', and to '… minimise the potential impact of not having a baby girl to take home with her; AB can be given a new baby doll soon after the procedure to keep with her'. The judge concluded that the '… trauma or upset of having a termination… (would pose) a lesser impact than having a baby'. Accordingly, the declaration that termination was lawful was made.

The Official Solicitor appealed this decision, and 3 days later the case was heard in the Court of Appeal. Their judgement was handed down on the 11th of July, by which time termination had not and would not take place given that in AB's circumstances, termination could not be made lawful by the Abortion Act since the pregnancy was now in its 25th week.

In upholding the appeal, the court found that in her conclusions, the High Court judge made no mention of AB's wishes or feelings or of the views of CD, the social worker or the Official Solicitor. They found, further, that the court is required to consider both (AB's) wishes and her feelings: 'The judge placed emphasis on the fact that AB's wishes were not clear and were not clearly expressed. She was entitled to do that but the fact remains that AB's feelings were, as for any person, learning disabled or not, uniquely her own and are not open to the same critique based upon cognitive or expressive ability. AB's feel-ings were important and should have been factored into the balancing exercise alongside consideration of her wishes'. The point was made that her mother and social worker knew AB better than any of the assessing psychiatrists instructed in the case. Their opposing evidence was not weighed against that of the doctors.

The Mental Capacity Act 2005 is founded, in part, on the basis that those who make decisions on behalf of a person who lacks capacity must respect and make the most of that person's autonomy and individuality. Even where a patient lacks capacity, her wishes and feelings not only must be considered; they can in some circumstances be determinative. It is to safeguard this principle that the Act provides that 'a person is not to be treated as unable to make a decision merely because he makes an unwise decision'.

CHAPTER 49

The Feasibility of a Covert Caesarean Section

NHST v JP [2019] EWCOP 23

At the late stage of 36 weeks' gestation, 1 week before proposed delivery, a hospital Trust's application for a covert caesarean section was heard in the Court of Protection. The judge could see no reason why it should not have been possible for the application and hearing to have occurred much earlier.

Notwithstanding the urgency, the court heard that JP, the putative mother, was 25 years old, with a mild to moderate learning difficulty which affected her cognitive ability. She was unable to make a decision as to mode of delivery because she did not understand the relevant information and was unable to use or weigh that information as part of the process of making the decision. Her health visitor and obstetrician described in evidence numerous attempts to convey information, but on each occasion her learning difficulty precluded her from using or weighing it. It was considered that an attempted vaginal delivery would be highly risky. The patient's usual response to pain and distress was to run, hide or become aggressive. If she escaped the hospital, she would likely suffer haemorrhage and infection. An escape attempt midway through labour would place the unborn child at great risk. An epidural would not be feasible, given her intolerance of needles. Routine blood tests had proved to be fraught, barely practicable.

What was proposed was a care plan based on a deceit. JP was to be asked to attend the hospital ostensibly for a monitoring visit, which in reality was a pretext for planned caesarean section. Oral midazolam would be disguised in a drink, and when that had taken effect the patient would be anaesthetised. The necessity for physical restraint was anticipated. Her cooperation might need to be enhanced with intramuscular ketamine. Once anaesthetised, a caesarean section and epidural would be performed; discharge to her residential unit was anticipated within 1–2 days. The plan also envisaged the newborn baby being removed from her after birth.

The risks and benefits of vaginal and caesarean delivery were identified and balanced. The clinicians involved asserted that vaginal delivery would be profoundly distressing and extremely risky for JP. The court was told that if vaginal delivery was commenced there was a realistic chance that JP would attempt to flee; ultimately, restraint, sedation and emergency anaesthesia and caesarean section would result. In face of this prospect, the covert care plan was seen by the court as the 'least worst option'.

There was, however, no doubt that JP made her wishes and feelings clear; she 'wanted to push it out' and 'did not want to be cut open'. This reason, and the foreseeable distress, distrust, anger and frustration caused by both the deception and the grossly invasive procedure against her will (in such a profoundly important matter) weighed considerably against approval of the treatment plan. Nevertheless, the judge found that '... the risks attendant upon an attempted vaginal delivery are so high that they plainly outweigh the risks linked to the proposed plan. The other disadvantages to JP of approving the proposed plan are not such to outweigh the overall medical advantages to her of approving it'.

The judge declared the covert caesarean section lawful. But at the same time, nature took its course. The day after the oral judgement, JP went 'off plan'. After the spontaneous onset of labour, JP gave birth to her baby naturally, without dramatic incident.

As the plainly delighted judge later put it: 'The capacity for individuals to confound judges' assessments is a reminder (to me at least) of the gap between probability and actuality'. He wished mother and baby well.

As we all know, clinical life can be equally confounding.

CHAPTER 50

Communicating Risk: Words or Numbers?

Ollosson v Lee [2019] EWHC 784 QB

We are becoming increasingly familiar with the identification of risks that need to be disclosed when seeking consent for treatment. Previously we relied upon an arbitrary numerical cut-off expressed as a threshold percentage to determine what we would or would not disclose. But we now are accustomed instead to asking ourselves what the reasonable person in our patient's circumstances would want to know. In addition, there may be specific topics that must be disclosed to the particular patient in front of you, reminiscent of the patient who wanted especially to know whether surgery on one eye could lead to loss of sight in the other (see the case in Chapter 26). For the moment, pinpointing risk is thus more or less straightforward. But how should we communicate these risks to patients?

Mr Ollosson suffered chronic disabling testicular pain after a vasectomy in 2012. He claimed that he was not given adequate information about the risk of this complication. Properly informed, he would have avoided undergoing the surgery. During a subsequent trial in the High Court, general practitioners (GPs) accustomed to performing vasectomy acted as expert witnesses. Both gave evidence as to what they would normally disclose prior to seeking consent for vasectomy. They agreed that risks such as infected haematoma, chronic scrotal pain and testicular atrophy should be disclosed, together with a 2% incidence of '… post-vasectomy pain severe enough to interfere with quality of life and daily activities and work'. In relation to practice in 2012, the experts agreed that as a substitute for setting out population risk as percentages, the use of words such as 'a small possibility of post-vasectomy pain which can be chronic' was commonplace, and an appropriate way of describing long-term pain.

Two urologists also provided expert evidence. Their approach differed from that of the GPs, since they both preferred to communicate risk using percentages. One viewed the use of a word such as 'small' as open to a variety of interpretations, failing to distinguish risks that were low in frequency from those which were low in severity. By contrast, expressing risk in percentages gives at minimum an idea of frequency. The other urologist acknowledged that reasonable patients would accept 1%–2% as a 'small' percentage, but reiterated the point that a small possibility should not hint at a small impact.

Recognising that Mr Ollosson had been extremely unlucky, the judge found nevertheless that taking all the facts of the case into consideration, the patient had been adequately informed of the risk.

Focussing on the adequacy of describing a risk as 'small', the court found this to be a satisfactory method of communicating risk. The judge accepted that the word means different things to different people, but 'small' remains a word that encompasses and satisfactorily conveys the level of risk involved. The judge was less comfortable with the use of the alternative adjective 'rare', although he did not give his reasons for this distinction. Perhaps because the word emphasises exceptionality and infrequency, tempting us towards a point where the entity described as 'rare' disappears altogether, in contrast to the way that 'small' indicates a modest but finite, undeniable measure of risk.

None of these semantics should obscure the obvious point that percentages can be used freely if the clinician so chooses, and this may well become necessary should a patient seek clarification of the small risk. The case provides *rare* judicial guidance that it is perfectly acceptable to describe the incidence of risks and complications in everyday words rather than using statistics while awaiting the patient's reaction prior to introducing numeric descriptions of the population risk, if need be.

CHAPTER 51

Stark Compulsion in Grave Circumstances

XHA v D [2019] EWHC 2311 (Fam)

The case of D, a 12-year-old girl, was recently reported. She had significant difficulty with food. Starting abruptly when she was 10 years old, D suffered unremitting symptoms ascribed to gastroenteritis. It had not been possible to identify an organic cause following detailed and extensive investigation. While much of the multidisciplinary clinical evidence pointed towards a behavioural component to her condition, some of the conventional indicators of anorexia nervosa were not considered to be present, and the court dealing with her case emphasised the necessity to keep an open mind as to her diagnosis. The court report made no reference to the use of the Mental Health Act during the description of her management. During a 1-month admission to hospital immediately prior to the court hearing, D had consistently refused to take food, and her life was considered to be at risk.

The court initially authorised reasonable and proportionate restraint to achieve 'force feeding'; it acknowledged just how distressing this was for D, her parents and those whose responsibility it was to achieve feeding in this way. Despite this regime, D continued to lose weight, more than 5 kg during the admission, leaving her at 27 kg.

The behavioural aspect of her condition touched on other areas of her clinical management. D resisted physiotherapy, mobilisation, dressing and toileting. One objective of D's current hospital was to identify a specialised unit more suited to deal with the totality of her presentation.

Such a unit was found, and the court's next step was to decide whether compulsory admission to and management within this unit was in D's best interests.

The judge was 'entirely satisfied that the treatment proposed is in D's best interests' and unusually spelt out what 'treatment' entailed.

That stark description of the compulsion to be employed in treating this 12 year old, separated from her family, is disheartening, spelling out severe interference with her freedom. D is to be observed 'at all times'; she will have daily showers; she will be encouraged to use the toilet; she will wear day clothing during the day. She will be fed by nasogastric tube, with restraint if necessary, and have a daily seating plan, prompted to move and discouraged from remaining for prolonged periods in one position. Regular and frequent physical examination will be necessary, together with observations that monitor her personal care.

Alongside all of this will be nursing and medical care, physiotherapy and both individual and family therapy. The overall emphasis, ironically, is to return D to independence.

The court recognised the 'distraction' caused by protracted litigation, and the clinical time spent in preparing for it. The judge sought to minimise this legal process, providing a fast track route back to himself, should the need occur.

Most clinicians can recall being 12 years old; we can feel our feet in D's shoes. Equally, all of us have at some stage been involved in clinical management entailing a degree of restraint or compulsion. So consider for one moment how D must feel, faced with enduring the regime authorised by the court. Those who understand eating disorders and are experienced in their management, tell us that this case simply demonstrates the reality faced by those suffering elusive and dangerous disease and that these measures are necessary; proportionate to the risks D faces if left without treatment, representing the least restrictive option available to provide her with effective therapy.

While that makes sense, it remains difficult for those who have no contact with these diseases to fully grasp their gravity, or the necessary draconian countermeasures. One can only hope that D recovers, ultimately believing that the right steps were taken for her.

CHAPTER 52

Going to Court Too Soon

Royal Bournemouth & Christchurch Hospitals
NHST v TG [2019] EWCOP 21

Mrs G collapsed in church with a subarachnoid haemorrhage followed by cardiac standstill. Resuscitation commenced between 5 and 7 minutes later, but she sustained extensive damage to her brain. There was no evidence that she was sentient. A vegetative state was diagnosed. Some 6 weeks later, neither her level of consciousness nor degree of responsiveness had improved. She remained intubated although required minimal ventilation. Around this time, the hospital sought a court declaration that continued intubation was contrary to Mrs G's best interests. On the 14th of February, less than 8 weeks after her bleed, the judgement was handed down.

The court found that her family believed that Mrs G responded both to the people who were close to her and to their prayers. The judge thanked the family for information concerning Mrs G's wishes, feelings, beliefs and values. This evidence comprised two threads. Firstly, Mrs G would have wished to stay alive, whatever the personal cost, if her living presence provided comfort to family members. Secondly, she had the '... utmost respect for life because of its intrinsic value and it was for no-one other than the Lord to take away'. The court found that her Catholic faith and belief in God remained a crucial part of her life. Summing up, the judge was satisfied that Mrs G's wishes, feelings, beliefs and values were '... plainly for the continuance of life'.

An expert neurologist appointed jointly by the hospital and the patient's representatives told the court that the best outcome Mrs G could hope for would be '... awareness of pain but nothing more than minimal consciousness at a very low level'. He said that her memory will '... almost certainly completely have disappeared and her previous personality will not emerge'. Nonetheless, the neurologist accepted that a tracheostomy could open avenues including specialist nursing care, perhaps within her own home, although she would be unaware of that fact.

The court found that personal dignity was not something writ large in Mrs G's life or thoughts. In addition, the court determined that pain was not a significant consideration, since she was not sentient, and if it did emerge, it could be treated.

The court was told that guidance by the Royal College of Physicians (RCP) indicated that in cases that are not the result of trauma, 6 months should elapse before the vegetative state is regarded as permanent.

During his balance sheet exercise, the judge reasoned that removing the endotracheal tube would bring an end to a process that conferred no significant benefit to Mrs G and excluded all possibility of pain and indignity. Against this was weighed continuation of Mrs G's life, recognition of her wishes, enabling her life to end at the behest of her God; the faint possibility of improvement; together with her ability (unwittingly) to continue playing a role in her family's life. On this basis, the court refused the application, finding that continued intubation was in her best interests.

But it was also made clear that should Mrs G remain in the same state for 6 months, a different decision might be made. Faced with the revelation of an RCP guideline that in these clinical circumstances 6 months should elapse before the diagnosis of permanence (of the vegetative state) could be made, it seems unlikely that a court would undermine that guidance by endorsing what amounted to a withdrawal of treatment less than 2 months after presentation. The hospital's case was contested by the family and the Official Solicitor (representing the patient). Despite the early severity of the injury, the wishes, feelings, beliefs and values attributed to the patient weighed heavily in favour of accepting the guidance at face value, and awaiting events. While courts encourage early applications when inevitability looms, such as progression towards parturition, they are unlikely to agree to definitive action contrary to the parameters set by national guidance.

CHAPTER 53

Best Interests in the Absence of Suffering

Barts NHSFT & Begum & Raqeeb [2019] EWHC 2530 Fam

Tafida Raqeeb was a 'happy joyful' 5 year old when, on a February morning in 2019, she complained of a headache. Shortly after, she stopped breathing; intracranial surgery revealed haemorrhage from a ruptured arteriovenous malformation. Following maintenance on intensive care and treatment of hydrocephalus, Tafida was clinically stable, dependent on artificial ventilation. She had suffered catastrophic damage to her brain. Her parents, Bangladeshi and committed Muslims, raising their daughter in the Islamic tradition, wished to take her to the Gaslini Hospital. In the absence of the criteria to fulfil a diagnosis of brainstem death, active withdrawal of treatment is not permitted in Italy. The Gaslini doctors had been provided with a full set of clinical notes and imaging, and a neurosurgeon, neurologist and intensivist reviewed her case. A subsequent videoconference with the UK hospital made it clear that the Gaslini doctors thought it highly unlikely that they could provide any treatment leading to an improvement in her condition. However, they offered palliative care indefinitely, including a tracheostomy and gastrostomy, although they envisaged that Tafida might eventually go home on long-term ventilation. The UK hospital made it clear that they did not agree to this transfer, believing it was contrary to Tafida's best interests. A UK paediatric intensivist instructed on Tafida's behalf concluded that the detailed transfer plan proposed by the Gaslini clinicians was appropriate and would be '... extremely unlikely to have any medical or welfare impact' on her. On the other hand, a consensus of expert evidence accepted that a long list of serious complications derived from Tafida's long-term care were inevitable.

Neither the expert instructed on Tafida's behalf nor the Children's Guardian appointed to represent her considered that prolonged sustaining treatment was in her best interests, largely because she could not derive benefit from continued life, although the latter accepted that in such a difficult case the court might reach a different conclusion.

The court reviewed a *fatwa* from the Muslim Council of Europe, and written representation from the Bangladeshi High Commissioner. Taking the *fatwa* (a written decision on a point of Islamic law given by a recognised authority in the field) and the High Commissioner's representations together, the court noted that any Bangladeshi national who consented to or participated in withdrawal of treatment from Tafida would be guilty of a criminal offence under Bangladesh law, and be liable to prosecution in that jurisdiction.

Having heard evidence from the hospital, parents and Italian doctors the judge found that Tafida has very severe generalised cerebral dysfunction. There is a consensus of medical opinion that it is not possible to exclude in Tafida some level of conscious awareness. But she shows no facial grimace to deep pain, does not cough or gag during endotracheal tube suction and has no withdrawal or heart rate response to painful stimuli. It is therefore likely that Tafida does not perceive pain.

The court noted an unchallenged report by the expert instructed for Tafida asserting that it was not uncommon for home-ventilated children to be admitted to a tertiary paediatric intensive-care unit during acute deterioration, and that '... in the majority of cases these children will recover to their baseline status and be discharged ... without the issue of withdrawal of life-sustaining therapy being addressed'.

As is usual in these cases, the judge employed the 'Welfare checklist' as an aide memoire to identify relevant factors that needed to be balanced against each other before he could reach a conclusion on where Tafida's best interests lay. Considering her wishes, feelings and emotional needs, characteristics relevant to her background that he derived from this enquiry, the religious context of her family life was plain to see. Using this approach, he found himself balancing evidence of Tafida's formative appreciation that life is precious and a wish to follow her parents' religious practice against little or no evidence that she would have to endure pain or suffering. Noting there was a prospect that Tafida could ultimately be cared for by her family at home in the same manner as other children in a similar position in the United Kingdom, the judge concluded that he was '... satisfied that if Tafida was asked, she would not reject out of hand a situation in which she continued to live, albeit in a moribund and at best minimally conscious state, without pain and in the loving care of her dedicated family, consistent with her formative appreciation that life is precious, a wish to follow a parent's religious practice and a non-judgemental attitude to disability'.

It is highly unusual to encounter a patient who is found by a court to be incapable of suffering. This case is an example of when few or no factors elicited by the Welfare checklist can be placed in the balance pan as a counterweight to the parents' wish for their child's life and faith to continue, however unlikely recovery might be.

CHAPTER 54

Patients Value Candour

No case

Since the Mid Staffs inquiry in 2013, two distinct species of candour have emerged. All eight regulators that scrutinise the clinical professions jointly set the threshold for us all; that *'if something goes wrong'*, we need, in effect, to have a dialogue with the patient, or their family, providing an explanation and/or apology, as appropriate. In most instances, sharing one's regret and sympathy that something has gone wrong for the patient may in reality be the most tangible human response to their distress. Our clinical duty is purely a professional one; the government refused to create a statutory duty that could be imposed on clinicians. Naturally, if we fail to be candid to patients, we may have to answer to our regulator.

Quite separately, the government's response to the Mid Staffs report was to impose a statutory duty (on all health and social care organisations that are registered with the Care Quality Commission [CQC]) requiring the organisation, in our case the hospital Trust, to be honest and open with patients or their families when something goes wrong *that appears to have caused or could lead to significant harm*. It is due to this statutory requirement that we have a now well-established mechanism for 'duty of candour'.

Failure to comply with duties usually results in a penalty, but this is the first year we have seen any levied in England. The CQC is empowered to issue fines, or embark on a prosecution, likely to inflict a grave wound on a hospital's reputation. The first fixed penalty notice for £1250 was issued to a hospital in Bradford for failing to issue a timely explanation and apology to the family of a child whose diagnosis had been delayed, and opportunities for hospital admission missed. The CQC's action did not relate to the clinical care, during which the child died; the fine was imposed solely for failure of candour.

In October 2019, a Cornish hospital was issued with separate fixed penalty notices totalling £16,250 for seven instances where the statutory duty of candour relating to safety incidents was not followed. These included cases of diagnostic delay, losing opportunities to manage deteriorating patients and medication errors. The Trust accepted that the communications with patients and family were, put simply, not good enough. On 13 occasions, the Trust failed to notify the patient or family of the available facts as soon as was reasonably possible.

More recently, the conclusions of an inquest asserted that a hospital in Lincoln had not carried out any investigation into the death of one of their patients, nor contacted her family in line with its duty of candour. The coroner was concerned that despite serious failures in the care of their patient, the Trust had not taken the opportunity to learn from them. A relevant medical witness (presumably requested by the court to attend) had not been sent to the inquest; nor had a Trust representative attended the inquest to hear the coronial conclusions.

As a result, the CQC proposed a prosecution of the Trust. Doubtless the hospital was relieved when the CQC could not adduce sufficient evidence, and the prosecution was not pursued. But it can be seen in all three actions that timely provision of information to patients and/or their families and engagement with all relevant actors in the course of safety investigations may well have avoided the scrutiny of the CQC.

Above all else, in each case the families involved would likely have valued contact with the hospital and exchange of information so they could have better understood how and why their loved ones were harmed; what was the 'something' that went wrong, and why did that happen? This really is not a difficult concept to understand, and to empathise with. The CQC, on behalf of patients, has put a price on candour.

CHAPTER 55

Informed Consent and Informed Dissent: Two Sides of a Coin?

Mordel v Royal Berkshire NHSFT [2019] EWHC 2591 QB

While we are all familiar with the need to ensure that patients are fully informed prior to consenting for treatment, the mirror-image duty of ensuring that their refusal is equally informed has been considered in court, after a mother claimed that her delivery of a baby with Down syndrome could and should have been avoided. Ms M, pregnant, presented herself at the booking appointment in the ninth week of pregnancy and accepted the offer of a number of tests which included combined ultrasound and serum screening for Down syndrome. Returning in her 13th week for the nuchal fold thickness scan, the sonographer recorded that Ms M declined this test; and for this reason, the serum screening element was in turn not performed. A second trimester 'quadruple' test was not offered.

Having heard the evidence, the court found that the sonographer had asked Ms M whether she wanted the screening for Down syndrome; that the claimant said 'no'; and that the sonographer had said, 'So we are not doing the screening then, we are just doing the dating scan and I will be checking the baby and making sure the dates are correct'.

The judge found that there was *'no real distinction between on the one hand consenting to and on the other declining a procedure in these circumstances'*, largely because the patient had either to accept or reject the offer of the scan on the basis that she was properly informed. (Risking the cliché, this might be expressed as consent and dissent being two sides of the same coin.) The court noted that the obligation to secure informed consent falls on the clinician rather than the patient, making clear that it was not the patient's reasons for acceptance or rejection that needed to be unpicked; 'rather, a gentle exploration is required of the patient's state of mind, conducted for the limited and specific purpose that she understands what is entailed'. In other words, the issue was the nature of the steps required to secure informed consent. These steps amounted to a limited number of questions to ensure that an 'unwarranted outcome' was avoided.

Summing up, the judge did not accept that the sonographer's role was limited to hearing the patient's acceptance or declination of Down screening. Rather, he found that she should have checked there had been a discussion at the time of the booking scan, that Ms M had been supplied with the relevant booklet, and that brief questioning was required to ensure that the patient understood the essential elements and purposes of scanning for Down syndrome. In doing so, the judge was echoing the evidence given by the claimant's expert witnesses. It would be interesting to know how this accords with current practice in obstetric sonography.

The judge's explicit approach was to ensure, in circumstances where the patient had provisionally accepted screening for Down syndrome, that she *still* wanted it. If she had dissented, the sonographer should then have sought confirmation, since the answer 'no' without more provided insufficient enlightenment of Ms M's attitude to Down screening.

In finding for the claimant, the judge found, based on the totality of the evidence that the ultrasonographer had not taken sufficient steps to ensure that the patient was making an informed decision. Without being in court, no commentator can seek to go behind that judgement.

But we are free to consider the notion that there is 'no real distinction between on the one hand consenting to and on the other declining a procedure'. If viewed as two sides of the choice coin, presumably the duty 'gently to explore' the state of the patient's mind applies equally to consent and dissent. Many treatment decisions start with a clear intuitive 'best' outcome, for example, that acquired blindness should be avoided. If after reasonable disclosure the capacitous patient chooses not to accept sight-saving treatment (the 'dissent' face of the coin), we will surely explore that decision. But if she chooses the 'consent' face, are we really gently to probe her state of mind because we have not been sufficiently enlightened by her answer?

This judgement may be applicable to screening decisions (the judge making it clear that the duty existed 'in these circumstances'). But we should be slow to extrapolate the idea that there is no real distinction between consent and dissent to the common clinical situation where there is a near-universally accepted 'best' outcome. On the other hand, genetic screening and/or termination of pregnancy remains contentious, with eminently reasonable citizens taking polar opposite views as to what is 'best'. In this and other situations where clinical equipoise prevails over investigation or therapy, we should all be cautious to ensure that both consent and dissent are informed.

CHAPTER 56

Parental Consent for Their Child's Deprivation of Liberty

In the Matter of D (A Child) [2019] UKSC 42

In 2015, the High Court was asked to consider the role of parents in depriving their children of liberty. Keehan J held that the parents of a 15-year-old boy 'D' with learning difficulties could provide lawful consent for his informal admission to a closed psychiatric unit. D had been diagnosed with attention deficit hyperactivity disorder when he was 4 years old, Asperger's syndrome at age 7 years, and Tourette's syndrome at age 8 years, together with a mild learning difficulty. Despite many difficulties managing his behaviour, D's parents looked after him at home until he was 14 years old, when informal admission to a hospital for assessment and treatment became necessary. The hospital provided mental health services for children and adolescents; D was accommodated in a building with an integral school. The external door was locked, and D was checked by staff every 30 minutes. The court was told that it was not necessary to detain D in order to treat him; thus the Mental Health Act 1983 provisions were inapplicable. D's parents provided consent for these arrangements.

Previous courts, both European and domestic, have held that a parent may impose (or authorise the imposition of) restrictions on their child's liberty. But such restrictions must not equate to a deprivation of liberty of the child. Keehan J declared that D's parents' consent nullified any assertion that he was being deprived of his liberty (in the legal sense that his human rights were being abused). He also declared that it fell 'within the zone of parental responsibility for his parents to agree what would otherwise be a deprivation of liberty; it was a proper exercise of parents' responsibility to keep an autistic 15-year-old boy who had erratic, challenging and potentially harmful behaviours under constant supervision and control'. Falling outside the Mental Capacity Act 2005 due to age, outside the Mental Health Act 1983 due to informality, and outside the Children Act 1989 since not premised on accommodation with the purpose of restraint, D benefitted from no formal safeguards to ensure that review of his detention is guaranteed, save for the goodwill of his parents and his doctors.

For this reason, Keehan J made it very clear that once D reached 16 years of age, he would come under the jurisdiction of the Court of Protection, and the question of whether his detention could be legitimised solely on the basis of his parents' consent would require further consideration.

It is accepted that D's detention was legitimised by the consent of his parents, acting in good faith; in much the same way as parents' consent makes lawful the major surgery and clinical interventions that doubtless have enduring effects on the child's welfare. But depriving a child of his liberty for an unspecified and unmonitored period has connotations of abuse of his human rights beyond those normally associated with physical treatments, and thus perhaps merits wider debate.

The case was duly reconsidered when D became 16 years old. He lacked capacity to consent to deprivation of his liberty, and Keehan J again heard the case, concluding that D's parents could not consent for the deprivation of a 16 year old, largely because Parliament had on many occasions distinguished the legal status of people who had reached 16 years of age from that of younger children. His decision was appealed, eventually heard in the Supreme Court. The majority judgement was handed down by Lady Hale '... that it was not within the scope of parental responsibility for D's parents to consent to placement which deprived him of his liberty. Although there is no doubt that they, and indeed everyone else involved, had D's best interests at heart we cannot ignore the possibility, nay even the probability, that this will not always be the case. That is why there are safeguards required by Article 5 (The Right to Liberty). Without such safeguards, there is no way of ensuring that those with parental responsibility exercise it in the best interests of the child...'.

With the advent of the Liberty Protection Safeguards, anticipated in October 2020, the role of parental consent will be overtaken by the new statutory arrangements for deprivation of liberty in 16 and 17 year olds. What remains to be seen is whether the Supreme Court's disinclination to entrust decisions involving liberty may be tested in younger children, and whether this 'erosion' of the scope or zone of parental responsibility may extend to decisions relating to medical treatment.

CHAPTER 57

Vulnerable with Capacity

DL v LA & Ors [2012] EWCA Civ 253

In the Matter of SA: LA v MA & Ors [2005] EWHC 2942 (Fam)

Patients who lack capacity are vulnerable because others, by definition, make decisions on their behalf. If decisions are made which are contrary to the patient's best interests, the incapacitated person may be defenceless. While vulnerability in this context is understandable, are there situations where a capacitous patient is nonetheless vulnerable to adverse decision-making?

This question was comprehensively answered by a court in 2012, which was considering the behaviour of DL towards his elderly parents. DL was in his fifties, and lived with his mother (90 years old) and father (85 years old). It was accepted that both his parents had capacity to decide whether their son should live in their house, and the degree of contact they should have with him. The Local Authority was concerned that DL had, over the preceding 7 years 'punished' his parents, behaving in an aggressive or intimidating manner towards them. He had physically assaulted and verbally threatened them, controlling their movements and their visitors. This included limiting the contact of his parents with healthcare and social care workers. Furthermore, there were consistent reports that DL sought to coerce his father to transfer the ownership of the house into his name, and he applied considerable pressure to have his mother, physically disabled, moved into a care home against her wishes.

It was clear that the protections provided by the Mental Capacity Act 2005 could not be used to assist the parents because they did not lack capacity. Could the inherent jurisdiction of the court protect the parents from their son, or did their capacity exclude them from being objectively 'vulnerable', thus outside that protection?

Relying on a previous landmark judgement (*Re SA* [2005]), the court emphatically concluded that the parents could be protected, since the court's authority could be applied to people with capacity who are constrained, subject to coercion or undue influence or for some other reason, disabled from making a free choice or giving or expressing real or genuine consent.

Elaborating, constraint was equated to 'some significant curtailment of the freedom to do those things which in this country free men and women are entitled to do'. With respect to coercion or undue influence, was defined as 'where a vulnerable adult's capacity or will to decide has been sapped and overborne by the improper influence of another'. This might entail the influence of a close and dominating relative, and where persuasion was based upon personal affection, duty, religious beliefs, social or cultural conventions or obligations. In these circumstances, only a very small amount of pressure, 'subtle, insidious, pervasive', may nevertheless be powerful.

The disabling circumstances alluded to were those reducing the vulnerable person's 'understanding and reasoning such as the effects of deception, misinformation, physical disability, illness, tiredness, shock, fatigue, depression, pain or drugs. Doubtless there are others'.

The judge in *SA* acknowledged that in many cases, a number of these features could be found, preventing free choice and genuine consent, while capacity is preserved.

The courts in both *SA* and *DL* were determined not to offer a definition of vulnerability, since that would limit or constrict the groups of 'vulnerable adults' who might benefit from legal protection. Nevertheless, the previous description gives a reasonably comprehensive guide as to how a vulnerable adult with capacity may present to clinical services. It would be most unfortunate if, by virtue of their technical 'capacity', vulnerable patients were put beyond the reach of judicial protection.

CHAPTER 58

Compulsory Treatment for Diabetes

The Hospital v JJ [2019] EWCOP 41

We often have to contemplate compulsory treatment in life-saving situations, such as the amputation of gangrenous limbs in patients lacking capacity. But dealing with the necessity of imposing daily treatment is paradoxically far more onerous, arguably impractical. In a case heard in the Court of Protection in 2019, JJ, a 24-year-old man living with his parents had presented for the first time in May with what proved to be type 1 diabetes. The court found that he had been a loving and engaging young man who had in his past wanted to 'look top to bottom' at his diagnosis of dyslexia but gave no other hint of any medical history.

At presentation JJ had received emergency treatment including intravenous insulin and had been discharged the following day, with a plan for education and support in the community. Regrettably, he refused to take his daily insulin at home and re-presented 2 weeks later, mid-May, with ketoacidosis. Despite admission, he declined treatment. No mention is made in the judgement as to the state of his capacity at this point, but restraint was employed to administer insulin.

JJ found this episode 'extremely traumatic', leading to a severe *adjustment disorder*. This manifested as acute anxiety, stress, hopelessness and sadness, leading him to respond in a disproportionately negative way to his diabetic diagnosis.

Now distrustful of medical staff and concerned about constraints to his liberty, JJ was nevertheless successfully treated, recuperating in the community. But following another rapid metabolic deterioration and significant weight loss he was admitted 2 months later. He would accept only sporadic doses of subcutaneous rapid-acting insulin; he would permit no other treatment for his persistent metabolic derangement. This prompted the court application which was supported by his parents, since his doctors were unable to provide what they regarded as optimal management.

Naturally, the court first needed to establish whether the presumption of JJ's capacity was rebutted. Liaison psychiatric evidence was adduced that an adjustment disorder met the criterion for a disorder of the mind and brain recognised by the Mental Capacity Act as the 'diagnostic' element of the test for incapacity. As to the functional element, the court was told that the manifestations of the adjustment disorder prevented JJ from weighing up the necessary information to make decisions about the treatment of his diabetes, including the consequences of consent or refusal.

On this basis, the judge found that JJ lacked capacity to make decisions relating to his medical treatment. But at the same time, that compulsory treatment, entailing restraint, would lead to further distress. The judge explored the feasibility of JJ participating in the hearing by telephone, offering him the possibility to do so shortly after he accepted a subcutaneous insulin dose; JJ did not feel able to join the hearing in this way.

A care plan for reasonable treatment of ketoacidosis was set before the court, which included necessary and proportionate restraint. JJ's parents hoped that following this judicial scrutiny, their son would be more accepting of the plan. Provision was made for the involvement of a psychiatrist specialising in diabetology (and, presumably, adjustment disorder) that would start within 1 week of the judgement being handed down. The court nonetheless implicitly acknowledged the difficulties and uncertainties the future held for JJ with insulin-dependent diabetes. All involved hoped that if he could 'fully understand, investigate, and familiarise himself … and perhaps with most difficulty, accept his diabetes', he might maintain a stable life in his community.

This case starkly exposes the limitations of the law. It is one thing to compel a person terrified of treatment to endure it in hospital while he is temporarily incapacitated. But aside from treatment of a mental illness, there is only a modest prospect of enforcing the daily grind of regular daily treatment of any of the countless chronic physical illnesses should the adult patient actively refuse to comply, whether or not they have capacity. It is a tribute to the cajolement of innumerable companions or carers that most of the time, while patients may grumble, they acquiesce to medication at home.

Although anathema to clinicians who strive to treat their patients well, we have little or no influence over their compliance. Litigation in this context is highly unusual.

CHAPTER 59

Approving Palliation

University Hospitals Bristol NHSFT v RR [2019] EWCOP 46

In August 2019, a hospital sought a court declaration that RR (a 20-year-old man) lacked the capacity to make decisions about the palliative care that he was being offered, and to approve the proposed plan.

At the time of the hearing, RR was at home, very poorly, with his father. He had suffered severe aplastic anaemia for 5 years. He had undergone stem cell transplant earlier in the summer of 2019, which had been unsuccessful, partly because he had not consistently followed the recommended treatment plan. Since then, RR had endured neutropaenic sepsis requiring intensive care; he had only recently been discharged.

He was expected to die within days or weeks.

RR's early life had been characterised by significant harm inflicted by both birth and then foster families. This then had perhaps been exacerbated by the regular use of non-prescription drugs. His eventual diagnosis included a complex mixture of emotional dysregulation and psychological conditions loosely formulated as Asperger's syndrome, autism and personality disorder. But he had eventually been successfully adopted and was greatly attached (and felt indebted) to his adoptive father. Both RR and his father had expressed a wish for a second transplant, although RR, reflecting on a 1% chance of success of a second transplant with a haploidentical donor, subsequently said he could not cope with a further period of inpatient treatment.

RR's capacity had been presumed until very recently, perhaps only questioned following the failure of his transplant a few weeks before the hearing.

The judge relied on an expert in psychiatry to explain how RR's mental illness might impair his capacity to make decisions about treatment, particularly in weighing relevant information in the balance and then communicating his decisions. RR's inability to manage distressing emotions and his pattern of maladaptive coping strategies was likely to make him unable to reflect on the aspects of his treatment that caused him particular distress, leading him to avoiding, not dealing with, them. As a consequence, it was 'very unlikely' that RR would be able to base decisions on relevant information disclosed to him. For these and other reasons, RR was found to lack capacity to make decisions about whether to have a second transplant.

Since he lacked capacity, it fell to the court to determine whether a second transplant would be in his best interests. Plainly, if it was not, then it would be unlawful to proceed with an intention to cure him.

The court was told that there was 'no real prospect' of a second transplant for a number of reasons; not least the specific risks of a haploidentical donor, including the discomfort and risks caused by cytokine release syndrome, the high risk of graft failure, and the morbidities of graft versus host disease. RR had said many times that he would not be able to tolerate a regime of 4 weeks' isolation together with the preparatory chemotherapy. To this was added the reality that RR 'would be a non-cooperative patient ... running the associated risks of death and toxicity from transplantation in addition to those of aplastic anaemia'.

Representing the incapacitated RR, the Official Solicitor, after careful consideration, concluded that '... the magnetic factors point to allowing (RR) as good a quality of time with his family and friends as possible'. For these reasons, the court concluded that a second transplant would not be in RR's best interests. RR died 48 hours after the judgement.

In the case of *NHS Trust v Y* (2018), the Supreme Court indicated that as long as the provisions of the Mental Capacity Act 2005 were strictly observed and followed, and there was no dissonance from any quarter, decisions about life-sustaining treatment did not need to come to court.

But if the 'way forward is finely balanced ... or there is a lack of agreement to a proposed action...', then these decisions should be placed before the court. Since RR had very recently been thought to have capacity and expressed a wish for further treatment, the 'lack of agreement' was a live issue, and it was plainly right to seek a judgement.

CHAPTER 60

Acquiescence; Not Consent

An NHS Trust v CX [2019] EWHC 3033 (Fam)

CX is 14 years old; 10 years ago he was treated successfully for his lymphatic cancer. Now relapsed with a different phenotype of the disease, stage 4, he faced three courses of chemotherapy, intervening assessment and ultimately stem cell treatment.

There was a 95% chance that blood transfusion would be required; CX and his mother are Jehovah's Witnesses. Neither would consent for CX to receive blood or blood products.

To provide CX and his family with an independent assurance that his best interests were being upheld, the Trust sought a declaration from the court that transfusion of blood was lawful. The court found that CX was Gillick competent to make decisions relating to his treatment, although it did not make a finding as to whether he was competent to refuse blood. The paediatric oncologists giving evidence to the court indicated that without the support of blood transfusion it would not be safe to proceed with the treatment of CX's cancer. The court was told that there were no case reports of patients who had developed these two different forms of cancer.

Both the child and his mother had made it clear from the outset that they would respect the law and any decision reached by a court, even if that did not accord with their personal religious beliefs.

CX had written to the court. He noted that this was a decision that he had taken on his own account; he was baptised into his faith after much thought and because he wanted to express his love to his God. He made it clear to the judge that were he forced to receive the blood, he would feel angry and upset '... because (the judge) would be forcing upon him something which he did not want'. CX queried why he was not offered blood fractions as an alternative to blood products, since his religion permitted treatment with blood fractions, which he could therefore agree to.

Set against this was CX's clearly expressed wish to survive his relapsed illness. This he had expressed to both the court and to his Children's Guardian, the latter appointed to present the court with an independent view of where his best interests lay. As the judge put it, '... CX himself has given voice to his own human instinct to survive his illness. He is clearly a courageous individual who has faced his current predicament with both dignity and obvious strength of character'.

Balancing CX's forcefully expressed wish to survive against the reverence with which he held his religious beliefs, the judge came to the conclusion that it was 'undoubtedly' in CX's best interests to undergo the planned treatment. Accordingly, a declaration was made that it was lawful to administer blood and blood products in the course of that treatment plan. The judge reminded the Trust of the importance of considering any alternative forms of management which might be undertaken to reduce the use of blood where feasible, so that CX's wish to receive '... as little (blood) as possible' could be honoured.

We have all observed the conflict that emerges when the patient's view of optimum treatment does not coincide with that of the clinician. This case can be distinguished by the eminent lack of conflict. Rather, CX's family took a measured and dignified approach to a grave difficulty forced upon them by a 14-year-old boy's cancer relapse. As in any family, his mother was possessed by an overwhelming wish for his life to be saved; she loved him dearly. Holding parental responsibility, she had the legal authority to consent for blood transfusion, but her religious convictions precluded this. Equally CX, Gillick competent, could provide consent, but was unable to do so for the same reason. The clinicians required consent, without which the transfusion would be unlawful, so could not proceed.

Happily the High Court, although not strictly providing consent, nevertheless was able to declare, under its inherent jurisdiction, that transfusion was lawful. The clinicians could proceed with treatment, CX will be given the chance of survival that he craves, and his mother will hopefully have her son restored to her, since she at the earliest stage indicated she would abide by the law.

It is unusual to see the legal transaction between a child, his Jehovah's Witness parent and his clinician set out so clearly. All involved want the patient to live; but the clinician needs consent, and the Witnesses are for honourable reasons unable to provide it.

By various methods, the courts can render the transfusion lawful despite the lack of consent from child or family. We wish CX well in his treatment.

CHAPTER 61

Making Clinical Legal Decisions

An NHS Trust & Ors v Y [2018] UKSC 46
Applications Relating to Medical Treatment: Guidance [2020] EWCOP 2

Mr Y was an active man in his fifties when he suffered a cardiac arrest and consequent cerebral hypoxia. He never regained consciousness. He was fed (clinically assisted nutrition and hydration [CANH]) through a gastrostomy, and over the following 3 months his doctors concluded that he was suffering a 'prolonged disorder of consciousness' (a term that courts have accepted as encompassing persistent vegetative and minimally conscious states). It was also concluded that if he were to regain consciousness, he would have profound disability, both physical and cognitive, and remain dependent on others to care for him. This prognosis was confirmed by a second opinion. His wife and children told the clinicians that Mr Y would not have wished to be kept alive if he had received that prognosis during the time preceding his loss of capacity. Accordingly, the family and clinicians all agreed that it would be in Mr Y's best interests to withdraw his CANH.

The question for the court was whether a court order must *always* be obtained in such situations, or whether, under certain circumstances, these decisions can be taken with the involvement of a court.

Twenty-five years earlier, the courts had considered two very different clinical questions. In *Re F**, the question related to whether sterilisation to prevent pregnancy (rather than to treat disease) could be performed on an incapacitated woman. In *Bland†*, it was proposed that CANH in a young man who had been in a persistent vegetative state for 3 years should be withdrawn. The House of Lords had made it clear in both cases that as a matter of good practice, a court declaration should be obtained (that the proposed treatment was in an incapacitated person's best interests) prior to the actions being taken.

This position was later consolidated in 2007 by a Court of Protection Practice Direction (PD 9E), addressed to lawyers and judges, that set out, among

---

* In re F (Mental Patient: Sterilisation) [1990] 2 AC 1
† Airedale NHST v Bland [1993]AC 789

other matters, a definition of 'serious medical treatment', and identified cases 'which should be brought to court'. The latter included proposals to withhold or withdraw CANH in patients in persistent vegetative state (PVS) or minimally conscious state (MCS) and in instances where, relating to incapacitated patients, proposals were being made involving organ or bone marrow donation, non-therapeutic sterilisation, or treatments and procedures requiring force or restraint. In 2017, the Practice Direction was revoked.

In considering Mr Y's case, the Supreme Court noted that decisions on withdrawing CANH are frequent and ubiquitous, taken consensually every day throughout the country in the best interests of patients with a wide range of neurodegenerative conditions, notably stroke and dementia. There could be no principled or logical reason to demand a court review of the tiny subset of patients with a 'prolonged disorder of consciousness' in the narrow MCS/PVS sense while blithely accepting the commonplace practice of withdrawal in other patients without recourse to the courts. Similarly, since CANH is seen as medical treatment, there can be no reason why its withdrawal should be seen as 'first amongst equals', there being no automatic recourse to declarations for withdrawal of antibiotics, ventilation or organ support.

For these and other reasons, the Supreme Court held that provided the provisions and guidance of the Mental Capacity Act 2005 were followed, and that there is agreement as to what is in the patient's best interests, then life-sustaining treatment, whether this is CANH or any other form of life support can be withdrawn or withheld without needing to make an application to the court.

Plainly, if there is any hint of lack of agreement or conflict of interest from any quarter, clinical or family, when the withdrawal of life-sustaining treatment is being considered, an application to court must be made. Equally, if in these circumstances at the end of the decision-making process the clinicians or family remain uncertain, because the conclusions on best interests are finely balanced, an application must be made.

This judgement marked a 'handing back' to clinicians of responsibility to make some decisions that for the last 25 years have been exclusively within the control of our courts. This redoubles the responsibility that clinicians bear to ensure that the Mental Capacity Act 2005 is understood and applied assiduously. But the handing back may prove to be illusory in the longer term. Perhaps anticipating clinical uncertainty as to where the threshold for court application now lies, the January 2020 'Guidance' sets out 'situations where consideration should be given to bringing an application to court', in respect of medical decisions that need to be made on behalf of incapacitated patients. This notes situations whereby *consideration must be given* to making an application and those whereby an *application must be made*. Essential reading.

CHAPTER 62

ABC: A Duty to Balance Conflicting Interests

ABC v St George's Healthcare NHST [2020] EWHC 455 QB

An eagerly awaited case has been decided. You may recall the story of ABC, whose father, XX, killed her mother, leading to his detention in a psychiatric facility. His clinicians tested him for Huntington's disease, which proved positive. He had capacity, and agreed to the testing only on the basis that his results were not shared with his family.

In the meantime, ABC fell pregnant. Her father's doctors knew about the pregnancy and wanted to disclose XX's diagnosis to his daughter; from the time of his diagnosis there would have been a window of 2 months during which termination of her pregnancy was feasible. XX refused to disclose, aware that such knowledge might have an impact on his two daughters' reproductive decision-making.

ABC discovered her father's diagnosis during a clinical visit when her baby was 4 months of age. Shortly afterwards, she decided that her father's diagnosis should not be disclosed to her sister, now in the early stages of her own pregnancy.

Four years later, ABC tested positive for Huntington's. Feeling that it was unfair to bring a child into the world in these tragic circumstances, she claimed that the doctors should have breached her father's confidentiality and told her of his diagnosis whilst she had a chance to choose whether she would undergo termination. In making this claim, she asserted that she was owed a duty of care by the doctors who also had a duty to respect her father's confidentiality.

The claimant told the court that the clinicians had a '… duty to balance the Claimant's interest in being informed of her risk of a genetic disorder against her father's interest in having the confidentiality of that diagnosis preserved'. The court noted that if on that basis the clinicians properly considered and balanced the conflicting interests; but decided not to disclose; they would have fulfilled their obligation, provided their conclusion not to disclose the information was reasonable. The judge concluded that it was just, fair and reasonable to impose a legal duty to balance ABC's interest in being informed against XX's interest in maintaining his confidentiality relating to both the diagnosis (and the public interest in maintaining medical confidentiality generally).

The court noted that no new obligation was being imposed on doctors or hospital trusts. Instead, the ruling simply '... recognised and ran parallel to a professional duty to undertake a proper balancing exercise which all the experts in the case agreed already exists'. The judge reflected that this duty would rarely act as foundation for litigation. At least in part because the legal duty to perform a balancing exercise would only arise in the rare circumstances when there was close proximity between the at-risk person and the clinician; and that reasonable doctors would often reach different conclusions as a result of the duty to balance.

As it turned out, the claimant's expert evidence accepted that if a proper balancing exercise had been performed for ABC/XX, reasonable and responsible clinicians could have decided not to disclose the diagnosis to ABC. This concession effectively ended ABC's claim that the newly established duty to balance had been breached. Furthermore, the judge reflected, 'It does seem to me that it would have been unduly harsh to hold (the defendant Trust) liable … for reaching the same decision as the claimant did in relation to her sister. Finally, the court found that the claimant did not prove that she would have undergone a termination if notified of the risk during her pregnancy. For these reasons, ABC lost her claim.

The judge could '... not see why genetic information should be treated differently from other information which reveals a serious risk to another person'. Accordingly, she gave a clear indication that she intended the duty to apply to any circumstances in which professional guidelines direct clinicians to consider the conflicting interests of their patient and a third party when serious harm is envisaged. The proviso is that there must be sufficient proximity, in other words a close relationship, with the non-patient (who will often be a family member) at risk.

Index

Printed in the United States
by Baker & Taylor Publisher Services